Physical Char
of the Beard

(from The Kennel Club

CW00403959

Body: Length of back comes from length of ribcage and not that of loin. Back level and ribs well sprung but not barrelled. Loin strong and chest deep, giving plenty of heart and lung room.

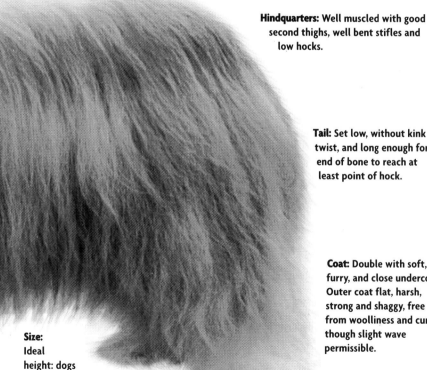

Hindquarters: Well muscled with good second thighs, well bent stifles and low hocks.

Tail: Set low, without kink or twist, and long enough for end of bone to reach at least point of hock.

Coat: Double with soft, furry, and close undercoat. Outer coat flat, harsh, strong and shaggy, free from woolliness and curl, though slight wave permissible.

Size:
Ideal height: dogs 53–56 cms (21–22 ins); bitches: 51–53 cms (20–21 ins).

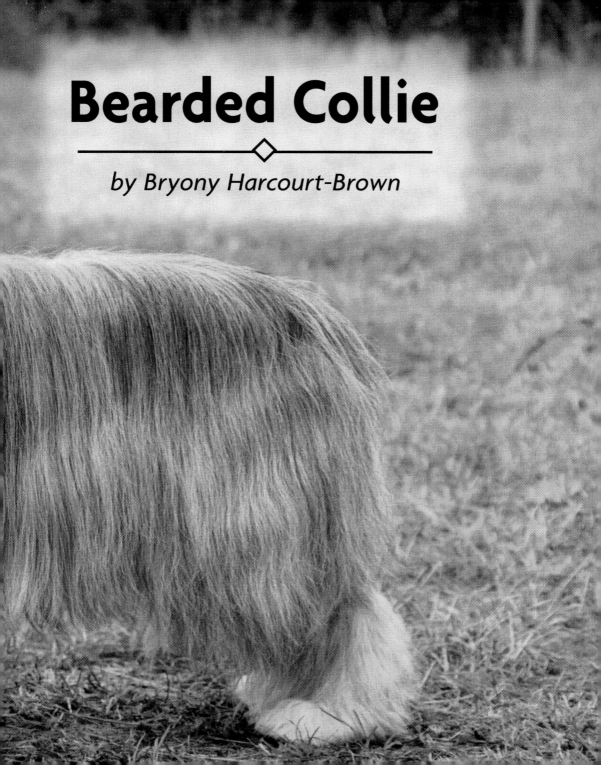

Bearded Collie

by Bryony Harcourt-Brown

Table of Contents

PUBLISHED IN THE
UNITED KINGDOM BY:

INTERPET
PUBLISHING

Vincent Lane, Dorking
Surrey RH4 3YX
England

ISBN 1-902389-35-2

86

PHOTO CREDITS

Norvia Behling
Bryony Harcourt-Brown
TJ Calhoun
Carolina Biological Supply
Doskocil
Isabelle Francais
James Hayden-Yoav
James R Hayden, RBP
Carol Ann Johnson
Bill Jonas
Dwight R Kuhn

Dr Dennis Kunkel
Mikki Pet Products
Phototake
Jean Claude Revy
Dr Andrew Spielman
Steven Surfman
Michael Martin Trafford
Karen Taylor
Alice van Kempen
C James Webb
Meryel Wood

Illustrations by Renée Low

112

Housebreaking and Training Your Bearded Collie
by Charlotte Schwartz
Be informed about the importance of training your Bearded Collie from the basics of housebreaking, and understanding the development of a young dog, to executing obedience commands (sit, stay, down, etc.).

136

Health Care of Your Bearded Collie
Discover how to select a proper veterinary surgeon and care for your dog at all stages of life. Topics include vaccination scheduling, skin problems, dealing with external and internal parasites and the medical conditions common to the breed.

140

Showing Your Bearded Collie
Experience the dog show world, including different types of shows and the making up of a champion. Go beyond the conformation ring to working trials and agility trials, etc., and learn what is required for your dog to participate.

Understanding the Behaviour of Your Bearded Collie
Learn to recognise and handle common behavioural problems in your Bearded Collie, including barking, jumping up, aggression with people and other dogs, chewing, digging, etc.

Copyright © 2000 Animalia, Ltd.
Cover patent pending. Printed in Korea.

Bearded Collie

Many people feel endeared to the Bearded Collie because of its 'shaggy mongrel' appearance. On the contrary, the Beardie is no mongrel; it is a purebred through and through with a long history as a working sheep and cattle dog.

HISTORY OF THE
BEARDED COLLIE

The Bearded Collie is very much the type of breed that many people feel they already know, simply because of their similarity to a lot of 'shaggy mongrel' types. Until comparatively recently, however, many people would not know the name of the breed when they met one and would often confuse the Bearded Collie with the Old English Sheepdog. Despite the similar shaggy appearance and herding heritage, the breeds are, actually, very different in body and head shape, general construction and overall balance.

The Bearded Collie has, in fact, a long history, in various guises but all rather similar to the dogs we still see nowadays. Grooming techniques may result in longer and, often, heavier coats but the basic shape and balance of the early Beardies are, or should be, still there.

The Bearded Collie originated in Britain as a working sheep and cattle dog. It is generally accepted that the Bearded Collie's temperament was ideally suited to the work of a drover, often covering great distances to drive cattle safely to market over rough terrain. This would

Although grooming techniques may result in longer, heavier coats, the basic shape and balance of early Bearded Collies are evident in examples of the breed today. This is the author's Ch Chriscaro Chrystal at Orora at three years of age.

certainly be borne out by the Bearded Collie's method of working stock, which typically displays a rough-and-ready attitude, nudging and nipping the heels and barging the beasts into order. This behaviour is still readily evident in present-day Beardies, given the opportunity.

> **DID YOU KNOW?**
> The Bearded Collie Club was formed and approved by The Kennel Club in 1955 to remain until the present time.

Some years ago, one of my Beardie bitches displayed her instinct with cattle in a most daredevil and courageous act, herding and removing some beasts that had broken out of their field and were making attempts to chase me on my pony. Despite my cries to her to come away, she took them to the far end of the field and rejoined me only when she could see we were out of any danger. This was a show bitch, long removed from working stock, who had never been tried with any form of work.

Beardies running with other dogs or, indeed, with their family members will also often display herding instinct, maintaining a constant eye on their 'charge' and constantly circling and checking the course of their playmates.

Various theories have been propounded as to the original breeds that formed the Beardie, but none of these have been satisfactorily proved due to a lack of written documentation. Nevertheless, it is generally accepted that a dog of hairy type with exceptional abilities with sheep and cattle and of a hardy disposition was highly prized in Scotland. These dogs may have derived from a number of sources, including some of the Eastern European breeds. However, it is most likely that the Bearded Collie predominantly gained ancestry from a number of native breeds and not from any one breed in particular.

Early Beardie types were known by a variety of names such as the Scotch Sheepdog and the Hairy Mou'ed Collie. In the South

Bryony Harcourt-Brown with her first Bearded Collie, a lovely chocolate and white, who converted the author to the Beardie fold.

DID YOU KNOW?
One of the 'breeds' considered by many to be an early Beardie cousin was called the Smithfield. Dogs named Smithfields, with a number of characteristics similar to Bearded Collies, are a highly prized working breed still being used for sheep and cattle by farmers in Tasmania. These dogs, like Beardies, give voice whilst working.

qualities have also repeatedly been attributed to them. These include their capacity for independent thought and their intelligence, allowing them to work without direction and bring home lost sheep without assistance. Another constant is the description of the dogs using 'plenty of voice,' an attribute that allowed the whereabouts of the dog to remain known despite its being out of sight. These qualities ensured that the Beardie type of worker was very highly prized.

Despite all the historical references to dogs of Beardie type throughout Britain, the Bearded Collie is generally known as a Scottish breed, and certainly it was from Scotland that the history is taken up in more modern and well-documented times.

Although still in existence, the Bearded Collie was largely forgotten in more recent years. The need for a long-distance drover had become all but obsolete with more modern

of England there were also dogs famed as drovers, of Beardie type, known as Smithfields. These were so named as they were used by drovers to take cattle to London's Smithfield market. The Smithfields were famous for their ability to find their own way home, passing from farm to farm along the way. Interestingly, there are still working dogs bearing the name of Smithfields in Tasmania today.

Other mention has been made of dogs known as the 'Barking Dogs' or 'Noisy Dogs,' which seem to have been of Beardie type and which possibly had been used by the Celtic people in early British history. Wherever mention of this type of dog is made, various

DID YOU KNOW?

In many parts of Britain, working Beardies were known as 'Barking Dogs' due to their habit of continually barking as they worked. You may wish to consider this if you are thinking of acquiring your first Beardie. It is a trait that they have not lost over the generations!

This is Ch
Mignonette of
Willowmead at
Orora who was
the Top Bearded
Collie in Britain
in 1975 and 1976.

This is Ch Mignonette of Willowmead at Orora who was the Top Bearded Collie in Britain in 1975 and 1976.

methods of sending sheep and cattle to market.

In 1944 Mrs G O Willison, a lady from England, wished to procure a Shetland Sheepdog from working stock and negotiated the purchase of such an animal from Scotland. In fact, she was sent a chocolate (brown) bitch puppy, which later proved to be a Bearded Collie.

Having researched the matter, Mrs Willison set about trying to breed from this bitch, Jeannie. The first litter, to a half-bred Beardie male, was not a success and none of the resultant puppies were retained. However, Mrs Willison was able to register Jeannie by a now-obsolete method that, at the time, allowed a judge to certify breed type and quality in a specific animal in order for it to gain Kennel Club registration. Jeannie was registered as Jeannie of Bothkennar.

Despairing over ever finding a suitable Beardie mate for Jeannie, Mrs Willison happened by sheer chance to meet a slate-and-white Bearded Collie dog and his owner on Hove Beach, Sussex. As the dog required a good home at that time, Mrs Willison acquired him and he was registered as Bailie of

DID YOU KNOW?

The first Bearded Collie to achieve the exalted title of Obedience Champion was Obedience Champion Scapa, by Ch Bosky Glen of Bothkennar out of Swalehall Martha Scrope. Scapa was owned and trained by Jenni (Cooke) Wiggins.

Bothkennar. Jeannie and Bailie produced their litter in 1950 and Mrs Willison kept four pups: three males, one named Bogle of Bothkennar, and a female.

A year later, Mrs Willison obtained Bess of Bothkennar from Argyll in Scotland. Bess was mated to Bogle and produced a bitch, Briery Nan of Bothkennar, who was to feature frequently on later pedigrees. Another outcross was Newtown Blackie; this dog, when mated to Briery Nan, produced Ridgeway Rob, a famous early male. Although there were other dogs brought in, the extent of the early available breeding stock was extremely limited. Consequently, it is probable that all modern-day Kennel-Club-registered Bearded Collies are descended from Jeannie and Bailie's original combination.

Miss K Suzanne Moorhouse, of the renowned Willowmead kennels, obtained Ch Willowmead Barberry of Bothkennar from Mrs Willison. Barberry's litter brother, Ch Wishanger Barley of Bothkennar, was owned by Miss Mary Partridge, famous for the Wishanger Beardies. Miss Partridge also obtained a bitch from Miss Moorhouse, Ch Willowmead My Honey, who, when mated to Ch Barley, produced Ch Wishanger Cairnbhan, another highly influential early stud dog.

In 1959 the first Challenge

Certificates were awarded at Crufts and the Best of Breed winner was Beauty Queen of Bothkennar, who quickly became the breed's first champion.

Miss Shirley Holmes, who was to become well known and respected for her Edenborough Beardies, obtained Ch Bracken Boy of Bothkennar, born in 1962.

Owing to ill health, Mrs Willison began to reduce her involvement in the breed, parting with many of her dogs, and in 1964 the highly successful Bothkennar kennel was finally disbanded.

Ken and Jenny Osborne obtained Ch Blue Bonnie of Bothkennar from Mrs Willison in 1963, who was followed by Ch

The Bearded Collie is a natural born runner with a great amount of endurance. In modern times, this energy translates into a bouncy, happy dog that needs lots of exercise to stay fit in mind and body.

DID YOU KNOW?
But for the tireless work of Mrs G O Willison, the Bearded Collie as we know it might not be around today. Mrs Willison is generally credited with the revival of the breed.

Bearded Collie

Two British-born champions, Ch Chriscaro Chrystal at Orora and Ch Orora's Laughing Waters.

Bravo of Bothkennar in 1964. Although Ken and Jenny already had Bluebelle of Bothkennar, Bravo and Blue Bonnie really became the foundation of the Osmart Kennel, a very famous kennel with many champions to its name. Probably the most influential of these champions would be Ch Osmart Bonnie Blue Braid, by Ch Bravo out of Ch Blue Bonnie. This wonderful blue male was to make a major impact on the breed, as was Miss Shirley Holmes's Ch Edenborough Blue Bracken, grandson of Ch

DID YOU KNOW?

A 1990s Beardie to be included in the International Sheepdog Society Register was Paul Turnbull's dog Blue, who was an excellent dog with sheep. Blue lived and worked in Rothbury, Northumberland.

Bracken Boy of Bothkennar and the top-winning Beardie for many years.

Other famous kennels, responsible for champions in 1960s' Britain included Cannamoor, Brambledale, Davealex, Western-isles, Tambora, Broadholme, Beagold and Chantala.

My own first Bearded Collies, obtained from the beginning of the 1970s, were from the Osmart and Willowmead Kennels. My Osmart bitch actually still carried unknown breeding on one side of her pedigree. I also obtained a bitch of working origins, although Kennel-Club-registered, from Scotland. These three, with a bitch by Ch Edenborough Blue Bracken, formed the foundation of my kennel. The bitch I bought from Miss Moorhouse became Ch Mignonette of Willowmead at Orora, who was Top Bearded Collie in Britain for 1975 and 1976. Mignonette was by Ch Wishanger Cairnbhan. When mated to Ch Osmart Bonnie Blue Braid, Mignonette produced Ch Orora's Frank, who is behind so many of today's dogs. Frank was Top Bearded Collie for 1983 and 1984.

Another dog carrying Wishanger lines was Mike and Janet Lewis's Ch Pepperland Lyric John at Potterdale. Lyric John, the first major Potterdale show dog, was to start a phenomenal show career for Janet and Mike. They have produced innumerable top-quality champions in the breed, including Brenda White's lovely Ch Potterdale Classic of Moonhill, the 1989 Crufts Best in Show winner, who was sired by Ch Orora's Frank.

BEARDIES AROUND THE WORLD

Although Bearded Collies were probably exported from Britain from the early part of the 20th century, the main exportation of Beardies from Britain seems to have begun in the late 1950s.

Beardies began to gain popularity around the world, generally being exported from the well-known British kennels. Many countries began clubs of their own, with Holland forming their breed club in the mid-1960s.

In 1969 the Bearded Collie Club of America was founded, with full status in the show ring being granted to the breed by the American Kennel Club in 1976.

By the mid- to late 1970s, Beardies were gaining popularity not only in Britain but also in many countries, with many quality British exports sent to establish kennels around the world. By the 1990s, many countries were breeding excellent Beardies descended from these original British dogs.

The Collie, or Scotch Collie, is the more familiar 'collie,' though the Bearded Collie is growing in popularity by leaps and bounds.

A testimony to Bearded Collie health and quality, here is Ch Orora's Frank, at ten and a half years of age, winning Best of Breed at Crufts.

The popularity of the Beardie has ensured that the majority of people nowadays have some idea of the look of the breed. Gone are the days when you have to explain to everyone you meet what a Bearded Collie is. However, due to its endearing looks, the Bearded Collie may be attractive to many people who would not actually enjoy living with a Beardie should they acquire one. Thus it is essential to understand the characteristics of the breed before you choose it for your family. Once you have made your choice and obtained your puppy, you have many years ahead in which to be satisfied or to rue your decision. Having said this, those of us who love these dogs do so for their many, many charms.

PHYSICAL CHARACTERISTICS

Beardies are medium-sized dogs, but they often seem much bigger due to their larger-than-life personalities. Although Beardies can seem quite small when curled up under a table, they become very large when jumping up at a friend in her best suit.

Males are much stronger in build and bulkier in coat than females, despite only a one- to two-inch difference in height at the shoulders. Consequently, males require substantially more

Beardies adore the company of children, especially well-behaved children. It is important to teach children to treat their dogs in a gentle manner.

of everything: more food, more grooming and often more strength in their owners' arms whilst their Beardies are still exuberant youngsters!

One of the major physical attributes of the typical Bearded Collie is its lack of exaggeration and its consequent soundness of structure. Because Beardies are built along the line of rather a basic dog shape, they probably are not so prone to some of the stresses and consequent structural weaknesses of some other breeds.

DID YOU KNOW?

There are only four main coat colours in Bearded Collie puppies. Despite all the adult shadings that occur, all Beardies are born either black, brown, blue or fawn, with or without (but usually with) white collie markings. All four colours may also come as tricolours, with additional tan markings on the cheeks, eyebrows, legs and under the tail. The pigmentation and eye colouring is determined by the colour of the coat.

17

A young black and white Beardie starting to feel at home in his new environment.

The movement of the Bearded Collie is, or should be, even, totally sound and smooth, with long reaching strides and a fluid effect. This is a most beautiful feature of the breed. The head and expression are also most individual, with a broad, flat skull, muzzle of equal length and enquiring, expressive eyes.

Another rather unusual aspect of the breed is the pigmentation.

DID YOU KNOW?

A Bearded Collie may get soaking wet to the touch, but rarely gets wet right to the skin unless being bathed. This is due to the thick double coat, the fluffy undercoat acting as an insulating waterproof layer. For this reason, Beardies are ideally suited to work in all sorts of weather conditions

The nose and lip pigment follows the birth colouring, being black, blue, brown or fawn. The eyes should also tone with the coat colouring and change as the dog grows. In fact, the whole colouring of the dog is constantly changing through time and is a most interesting aspect of the breed. For instance, the brown Beardie puppy is quite chocolate at eight weeks, only to change gradually to pale fawn, sometimes almost to white, by about 12 to 16 months. The coat may then darken gradually again until the full adult coat is gained by about four or five years of age. In the case of browns particularly, the constant growth of coat means that the colour is always changing—throughout the dog's life and in different areas of the coat at any one time. At the same time, the eyes are constantly changing in colour as well. Eyes can change from an almost yellow colour as a youngster to perhaps a deep amber or copper as a mature dog. In this way the dog really provides an ever-changing level of attractiveness. Perhaps to a lesser degree, the other colours undergo the same changes. For example, the born black will lighten and darken at similar times, probably never really to regain its original blackness. Blues will also lighten to nearly silver at around 12 to 16 months and then gradually regain much of their birth colour by maturity. Born fawns are perhaps

the least common of all the colours; this is probably because they generally, although not always, have a somewhat less attractive eye colouring, which can be rather pale. Additionally, there are more constraints on fawns in breeding; when choosing a mate, pigmentation and colour are big considerations. Nonetheless, the fawn coat colouring is very lovely, being mushroom in hue as a baby and often having a frosting of white as the coat matures. A fawn with good eye colouring is a beautiful dog.

DID YOU KNOW?
Bearded Collies have a highly developed sense of hearing and can become quite distressed by strangely pitched noises. Many Beardies are fearful of gunfire, jet planes or fireworks for this reason. The problem can become quite acute in the middle-aged dog who may be losing its hearing slightly; the dog seems unable to make sense of strange, sudden noises. Later in life, perhaps as the dog loses more hearing, the problem often lessens.

Beardie puppies love outdoor recreation, especially picnics with young friends.

19

DID YOU KNOW?

The Bearded Collie should have coat between the pads of its feet. This helps to insulate the dog's feet when working in cold conditions.

The Bearded Collie is a very attractive breed, capable of a most dramatic transformation from scruffy mongrel type to stylish show dog with comparatively little effort. Personally, I find this to be one of the breed's most endearing qualities.

PERSONALITY

Although hugely rewarding to so many families, to some the Bearded Collie would not be the easiest breed to live with. Beardies have strong and exuberant personalities. They are loving and giving dogs…and they are prepared to love and give at all times, whether you are of the same frame of mind or not. The typical Bearded Collie is not usually a one-person dog, it is a family dog.

Beardies are not suitable at all for people who cannot spend a lot of time with them. It would not be fair to leave a Beardie in the

The brown Bearded Collie is quite chocolate as a young puppy, lightens to almost white, and then darkens gradually again until the full adult coat grows in at around four or five months of age. This brown male is three years old.

house all day whilst you go to work. Beardies need companionship and entertainment or they make their own fun (aka mischief). It is perfectly possible for a Beardie to dismantle a home if left without entertainment for long periods. Beardies find it impossible to curtail their natural *joie de vivre* simply at the will of their owners, despite the fact that they are intensely eager-to-please dogs. This breed is suited to the energetic, outdoor-loving owner, perhaps with children around the ages of, say, eight years or so and older. The whole family needs to be committed to the dog and to spending time with it.

Beardies find it extremely hard not to bounce, jumping up at you at the most inopportune times. Although with training their jumping up can be curtailed, I find it can never be wholly eradicated!

Beardies can have penetrating and, sometimes, excessive barking abilities. Please keep this in mind if you have peace-loving neighbours!

Having said all this, many, many people adore the breed. Beardies are hugely rewarding and cheer you up when you are most down. They are very trainable and quick to learn basic obedience. Beardies are bright and attentive learners, but they can become bored quickly. Training sessions should be kept short and not too intense.

Beardies are generally excellent with children. This depends, of course, on the individual dog and also on the children in question. Children should always be expected to behave responsibly with dogs. No dog should be left unsupervised with young children but, as dogs go, Beardies are generally consid-

Black-born Bearded Collies will lighten and darken as they grow older but will most likely never regain their original blackness. This is a black-born male at seven months.

DID YOU KNOW?
Many Beardies are highly skilled escape artists, being capable of scaling an 8-foot fence if they wish to. Others simply never consider this option at all and are happy to sit behind a 4-foot fence without ever once considering hopping over it. It is important that any area, such as your garden, in which your Beardie is to have unrestrained access, is properly secure.

ered to be one of the more suitable breeds for families with children. My own dogs took on my children, having not had any experience with babies for generations, with pride and devoted love. Beardies are often able to temper their exuberance, in a way they find totally impossible at other times, to a level suitable for children!

It is important to encourage children not to treat the Bearded Collie as another child, something that may bring out the worst in a Beardie. The dog will often take the initiative and build upon the 'child' game to excess, for

instance, when playing chasing games. Beardies often have to be taught when to stop. Likewise, Beardies will sometimes pick up characteristics of other breeds and copy them, so don't let your Beardie have access to observing aggressive or unpleasant types in the dog world.

Beardies need plenty of exercise and, once they are offered it, will generally insist upon it on a regular basis. Walks on the lead are fine, but in my opinion an adult Beardie really needs lots of free running. Beardies are prepared to run endlessly, loving to chase a ball or

The Bearded Collie makes an excellent choice for families with children.

play with another dog. I feel this is definitely the best and easiest way to exercise your Beardie and to keep it happy and healthy. The Beardie is not the type of dog to let you out of this exercise commitment in wet weather, so be prepared with suitable all-weather gear.

Fortunately, the typical Beardie coat is ideally suited to all types of weather. The coat insulates against heat and protects the body against damp and cold, which can rarely penetrate the thick undercoat. An added advantage is that the coat sheds dirt, as the mud dries and the sand drops off, to leave a fairly clean dog and a rather dirty floor.

With all this energy and ability to bounce, the Beardie has a natural ability when it comes to agility competition. A lot of fun can be had with a Beardie and a supervised agility course. Remember that a young dog

should be introduced gradually and that agility is more stressful on the dog's limbs than normal exercise. It is sensible to ask your veterinary surgeon for an opinion about your dog's suitability for agility.

HEALTH CONSIDERATIONS
Considering that the Bearded Collie was revived from near obscurity by Mrs Willison from breedings involving very few dogs, all breed members today descend from a fairly narrow gene pool. At the time, Mrs Willison had access to so few animals upon which to found not only her kennel but also, as it turned out, the whole future of the breed. These original dogs were registered by means of a judge authenticating the breeders' claims that the dogs were Bearded Collies. This method was phased out by The Kennel Club in the

When playing with other dogs, Bearded Collies have a tendency to pick up behaviours of other breeds and copy them. Make sure that your Beardie only spends time with well-mannered dogs.

As a puppy, the Beardie is an energetic bundle that loves to play. This youngster awaits his master's entry into his game. This is the canine play stance.

early 1970s and so the option of bringing in further unregistered dogs, with the resultant input of fresh breeding, was no longer available. Basically, all modern-day Bearded Collies could be considered to be quite closely linked genetically.

Consequently, there is little scope for very close breeding in Bearded Collies, and close breeding naturally increases the chance of defects or faults occurring in the puppies.

There are various terms used in dog breeding. Linebreeding, the most commonly employed method of breeders, is drawing on one or more (hopefully superior) dogs in the background of a five-generation pedigree in an effort to obtain the dogs' best points and pass them on to the puppies. Close linebreeding might be a grandfather to granddaughter combination, for instance. Inbreeding, a method frowned upon by some breeders, would be

All dogs communicate with one another, regardless of breed. This black collie seems to be giving the Beardie a fair warning by showing his teeth and growling.

defined by persistent very close family breeding such as father/daughter, half-brother/half-sister or brother/sister, for instance. Dogs can also be inbred where the same ancestors repeatedly occur in the background of the pedigree.

Close family breeding should only be attempted with extreme care, if at all, in Bearded Collies. At all times, pedigrees are likely to carry some dogs a few times, but excessively close breeding can only increase the probability of defects appearing in the puppies. For this reason, breeding Bearded Collies should not be undertaken lightly and should be undertaken only by people with full

knowledge of the backgrounds of the dogs in the pedigree.

Having said this, Bearded Collies are blessed with remarkably few of the more well-known inherited defects that affect many breeds. There are, however, various conditions which, although not necessarily breed-specific, may be of interest to the prospective puppy owner.

HIP DYSPLASIA

This is a distressing condition affecting the hip joint. The hip is a ball-and-socket joint that may be affected by the socket's not being deep enough or the ball's being incorrectly formed, and thus a general laxity of the hip. Often, as

Beardies make excellent partners for ballroom dancing, especially for children that are their own height.

a consequence, arthritic changes occur in the joint. This is a painful condition and the dog will suffer lameness and pain if arthritis is present. It is possible to x-ray potential breeding stock for signs of this disease and most breeders will do so. The x-rays, taken by a veterinary surgeon and usually with the dog under anaesthetic, are sent to the British Veterinary Association (BVA)/Kennel Club scheme and examined by two veterinary surgeons from a panel according to a specified formulation. A scoring system allows breeders to ascertain the severity, or otherwise, of the dog's condition.

Socialise your Bearded Collie with all types of other creatures, not just dogs. This Beardie is getting acquainted with a rabbit. From his stance, you can tell that he is ready for play.

25

The maximum score in Britain is 53 for each hip and the minimum is 0. Although there are affected dogs in the breed, we are fortunate that Beardies as a breed have a relatively low average hip score, currently around 10 as a combined score for both hips, meaning that they have relatively good hips as a breed. This is even more encouraging as many, many Beardies are routinely x-rayed. Countries have differing methods of scoring; in some countries it is required that dogs are x-rayed and that their hip status is within a specified range prior to breeding.

Even the greatest care by the breeder will not ensure that resultant puppies are free from hip dysplasia, so a certain amount of risk is involved, as it is with the purchase of any dog.

UNILATERAL OR BILATERAL CRYPTORCHIDISM

In some male Bearded Collies, one or both of the testicles will fail to descend into the scrotum and will remain in the inguinal region or in the abdominal cavity. I find it should be possible to feel both testes in the male dog from an early age (six to eight weeks or less), although some experience will be necessary in checking males. If the testes cannot be felt

The author wishes to thank Dr Malcolm Willis and Mrs V Stockman, MRCVS, for supplying information on hip dysplasia.

DO YOU KNOW ABOUT HIP DYSPLASIA?

Hip dysplasia is a fairly common condition found in purebred dogs. When a dog has hip dysplasia, its hind leg has an incorrectly formed hip joint. By constant use of the hip joint, it becomes more and more loose, wears abnormally and may become arthritic.

Hip dysplasia can only be confirmed with an x-ray, but certain symptoms may indicate a problem. Your dog may have a hip dysplasia problem if it walks in a peculiar manner, hops instead of smoothly runs, uses his hind legs in unison (to keep the pressure off the weak joint), has trouble getting up from a prone position or always sits with both legs together on one side of its body.

As the dog matures, it may adapt well to life with a bad hip, but in a few years the arthritis develops and many dogs with hip dysplasia become cripples.

Hip dysplasia is considered an inherited disease and can usually be diagnosed when the dog is three to nine months old. Some experts claim that a special diet might help your puppy outgrow the bad hip, but the usual treatments are surgical. The removal of the pectineus muscle, the removal of the round part of the femur, reconstructing the pelvis and replacing the hip with an artificial one are all surgical interventions that are expensive, but they are usually very successful. Follow the advice of your veterinary surgeon.

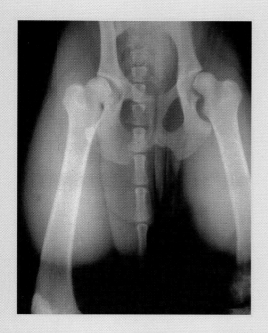

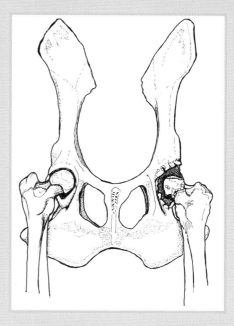

The illustration above shows a healthy hip joint on the right and an unhealthy hip joint on the left. Hip dysplasia can only be positively dianosed by x-ray, Bearded Collies manifest the problem when they are between four and nine months of age, the so-called fast-growth period.

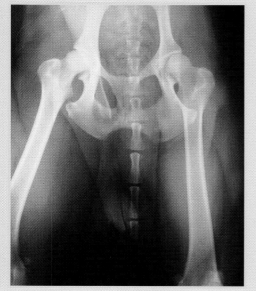

Compare the two hip joints and you'll understand dysplasia better. Hip dysplasia is a badly worn hip joint caused by improper fit of the bone into the socket. It is easily the most common hip problem in Bearded Collies.

at this age, I believe that there is a high chance that the dog will not be 'entire' at maturity. Beardie males should normally have both testes fully descended into the scrotum by, at the latest, around six months of age, although it is possible for this to occur later. If one or both of the testes remain in the abdominal cavity, the dog is termed unilaterally or bilaterally cryptorchid, (the term *cryptos* meaning hidden). Your veterinary surgeon will probably advise castration of the dog, as testicular cancer is more common in these dogs since the testicle can reach an abnormally high temperature inside the body. It is possible for a male Beardie with only one descended testicle to sire a litter; however, these dogs should not be used at stud as the condition is often inherited.

UMBILICAL HERNIAS

These are formed at the sight of the attachment of the umbilical cord to the puppy. A weakness of the abdominal wall allows the protrusion of a small amount of tissue under the skin. This is not an uncommon problem and can occur in any breed. Small umbilical hernias rarely cause a problem to the dog. Some veterinary surgeons may advocate the repair of the hernia, which involves a relatively simple procedure under anaesthetic. Larger hernias are more serious and definitely require repair. Occasionally the hernia will involve the abdominal contents (covered externally with skin). In this instance, the puppy should have had effective repair and recovery whilst still with the breeder. The condition is generally

Bearded Collies are loving and giving dogs. The typical Bearded Collie is not usually a one-person dog but a family dog.

Beardies are very devoted to their owners and like to accompany them wherever they go.

considered to be inherited and dogs affected to any but the most minor degree are, therefore, really not suitable for breeding.

MOUTHS

Over recent years many breeders have noticed an increasing problem with mouths in the breed. A Bearded Collie should have a scissor bite; that is, the upper incisors closely overlapping the lower incisors. Adult dogs should possess the correct bite, and many puppies will have this bite by the time they leave the breeder. Some will have a slightly overshot bite (the top incisors overlapping the bottom incisors with a gap between the two sets of teeth), but very often a slightly overshot bite will correct with age and is a normal aspect of puppy growth. However, some overshot mouths appear not to correct as the dog grows. An increasing number of dogs have rather narrow bottom jaws, which results in the lower canine teeth's grazing, or protruding into, the tissue of the upper gums. This condition may improve with age; if not, the problem canine tooth can be removed by a veterinary surgeon. Although not an ideal situation at all, the procedure is necessary and relatively simple. Dogs requiring this treatment are not suitable for show or breeding. Hopefully this problem will be corrected by breeders' only selecting dogs with perfect mouths since puppyhood for their breeding programmes.

The standard of any breed is the description of the ideal dog of that breed. All typical specimens of the Bearded Collie will have many attributes described in the standard; the best Bearded Collies, in show terms, will be those that conform the most closely to the standard in all respects.

Having said this, the standard has to be interpreted. In this lies the potential variation—since the interpreters of the standard are people, they will often see the dog in differing guises!

I thought, when I was a 13-year-old child, that my first Bearded Collie adhered remarkably closely to the breed standard, so much so that I felt she couldn't fail to win Best in Show at any show we cared to enter. In fact she was not, in show terms, one of the world's best Beardies (although she did end up as grandmother of one of my first champions). Even if judges had been foolish enough to see her as I did, they rarely had a chance to since she invariably left the ring as we ran around it, with me in compulsory attendance!

Nevertheless, experienced and knowledgeable judges are used to reading and interpreting standards and do so regularly in order to obtain a blueprint by which to judge the breed.

The Bearded Collie's coat is strong and shaggy, free from woolliness and curl. It should not be trimmed in any way if you are planning to show your dog.

THE KENNEL CLUB STANDARD FOR THE BEARDED COLLIE

General Appearance: Lean active dog, longer than it is high in an approximate proportion of 5 to 4, measured from point of chest to point of buttock. Bitches may be slightly longer. Though strongly made, should show plenty of daylight under body and should not look too heavy. Bright, enquiring expression is a distinctive feature.

Characteristics: Alert, lively, self-confident and active.

Temperament: Steady, intelligent working dog, with no signs of nervousness or aggression.

Head and Skull: Head in proportion to size. Skull broad, flat and square, distance between stop and occiput being equal to width between orifices of ears. Muzzle strong and equal in length to distance between stop and occiput. Whole effect being that of a dog with strength of muzzle and plenty of brain room. Moderate stop. Nose large and square, generally black but normally following coat colour in blues and browns. Nose and lips of solid colour without spots or patches. Pigmentation of lips and eye rims follows nose colour.

Eyes: Toning with coat colour, set widely apart and large, soft and affectionate, not protruding. Eyebrows arched up and forward but not so long as to obscure eyes.

Ears: Of medium size and drooping. When alert, ears lift at base, level with, but not above, top of skull, increasing apparent breadth of skull.

Mouth: Teeth large and white. Jaws strong with a perfect, regular and complete scissor bite preferred, i.e. upper teeth closely overlapping lower teeth and set square to the jaws. Level bite tolerated but undesirable.

Neck: Moderate length, muscular and slightly arched.

Bad example. Lack of eyebrows and hair obscuring eyes.

Good example. Eyes are soft and affectionate; eyebrows are arched up and forward.

Forequarters: Shoulders sloping well back. Legs straight and vertical with good bone, covered with shaggy hair all round. Pasterns flexible without weakness.

Body: Length of back comes from length of ribcage and not that of loin. Back level and ribs well sprung but not barrelled. Loin strong and chest deep, giving plenty of heart and lung room.

Hindquarters: Well muscled with good second thighs, well bent stifles and low hocks. Lower leg falls at right angle to ground and, in normal stance, is just behind a line vertically below point of buttocks.

Feet: Oval with soles well padded. Toes arched and close together, well covered with hair, including between pads.

Tail: Set low, without kink or twist, and long enough for end of bone to reach at least point of hock. Carried low with an upward swirl at tip whilst standing or

Muzzle too short.

Correct muzzle.

walking, may be extended at speed. Never carried over back. Covered with abundant hair.

Gait/Movement: Supple, smooth and long-reaching, covering ground with minimum of effort.

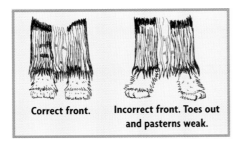

Correct front.   Incorrect front. Toes out and pasterns weak.

Coat: Double with soft, furry, and close undercoat. Outer coat flat, harsh, strong and shaggy, free from woolliness and curl, though slight wave permissible. Length and density of hair sufficient to provide a protective coat and to enhance shape of dog, but not enough to obscure natural lines of body. Coat must not be trimmed in any way. Bridge of nose sparsely covered with hair slightly longer on side just to cover lips. From cheeks, lower lips and under chin, coat increases in length towards chest, forming typical beard.

Colour: Slate grey, reddish-fawn, black, blue, all shades of grey, brown and sandy with or without white markings. When white occurs it appears on foreface, as a blaze on skull, on tip of tail, on chest, legs and feet and, if round the collar, roots of white hair should not extend behind shoulder. White should not appear above hocks on outside of hindlegs. Slight tan markings are acceptable on eyebrows, inside ears, on cheeks, under root of tail

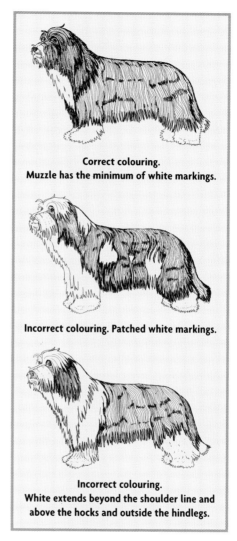

**Correct colouring.
Muzzle has the minimum of white markings.**

Incorrect colouring. Patched white markings.

**Incorrect colouring.
White extends beyond the shoulder line and above the hocks and outside the hindlegs.**

Correct tail.   **Incorrect tail; set too high and curled.**

and on legs where white joins main colour.

Size: Ideal height: dogs 53–56 cms (21–22 ins); bitches: 51–53 cms (20–21 ins). Overall quality and proportions should be considered before size but excessive variations from the ideal height should be discouraged.

Faults: Any departure from the foregoing points should be considered a fault and the seriousness with which the fault should be regarded should be in exact proportion to its degree.

Note: Male animals should have two apparently normal testicles fully descended into the scrotum.

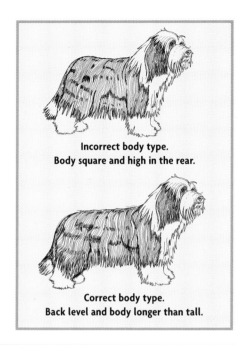

Incorrect body type.
Body square and high in the rear.

Correct body type.
Back level and body longer than tall.

This Bearded Collie did very well at Crufts in 1999. A proud owner shows off her champion.

How the dam of your puppy measures up to the standard will be a fair indication of how well your puppy will conform. Quality begets quality, thus it is important to see the dam and sire, if possible, of your puppy before making your selection.

BEARDED COLLIE

Once you have chosen your breed, you need to choose a breeder. It is vital that you obtain your puppy from a reputable source. Although one can never provide a guarantee with a puppy, a reputable breeder will have done everything possible to ensure that the puppy you buy will be a happy, healthy addition to your family. Reputable breeders will generally perform any necessary tests on their breeding stock to ensure, as far as they can, that they do not have any hereditary defects. Although Beardies are remarkably free of proven problems, breeders are recommended to x-ray their breeding stock for hip dysplasia.

Once you have located a suitable breeder, go and see their dogs and discuss the breed with them. Be prepared for them to try to put you off Beardies and listen to what they say. They know the breed and will have a good idea if it is not the one for you.

Be honest—don't tell a breeder that you will want to show your dog if you have no intention of doing so. It is unfair to try to buy the best potential show prospect and never to take it to any shows. Breeders who show

their dogs like to see them in the show ring. Most puppies in the litter will look the same to you, regardless of their show potential,

DID YOU KNOW?

Unfortunately, when a puppy is bought by someone who does not take into consideration the time and attention that dog ownership requires, it is the puppy who suffers when he is either abandoned or placed in a shelter by a frustrated owner. So all of the 'homework' you do in preparation for your pup's arrival will benefit you both. The more informed you are, the more you will know what to expect and the better equipped you will be to handle the ups and downs of raising a puppy. Hopefully, everyone in the household is willing to do his part in raising and caring for the pup. The anticipation of owning a dog often brings a lot of promises from excited family members: 'I will walk him every day,' 'I will feed him,' 'I will housebreak him,' etc., but these things take time and effort, and promises can easily be forgotten once the novelty of the new pet has worn off.

and they will certainly make just as nice family companions. Likewise, the breeder has a responsibility to tell you if the puppy has some aspect (usually termed a show fault) that would render the dog totally unsuitable for entering at a show. For instance, mis-marking, which would be too much white or white markings in an unaccept-able place, e.g. on the back or on the outer thighs of the dog, would be considered a fault in the show ring.

If you have a particular feeling for one colour only, you should stipulate this since you are hopefully going to live with the dog for many years. However, don't forget that the coat colour is going to change a lot over those years.

Once the litter is born, try to get to see the puppies at a fairly young age. Most breeders will be happy to show you the puppies after around five to six weeks of age, once they have begun to be weaned from the dam. It would probably not be sensible for you to try to definitely choose the puppy at this stage since they change so much and their temperaments cannot be assessed at such a young age.

When it comes to the time to choose your puppy, be guided by the breeder. He or she will have much more experience, especially in evaluating individual tempera-

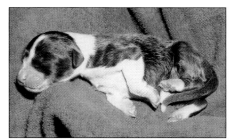

This newborn Bearded Collie pup has not even opened his eyes yet.

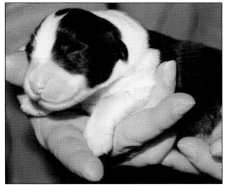

Most breeders will not show you their puppies until they are at least three or four weeks of age. This baby is only a few days old and is not ready to be exposed to strange people or other dogs.

The best time to start thinking about which puppy you want is around four to six weeks of age. If possible, it is best to see the dam as well before making a decision.

ments in relation to prospective owners. A lot of people are attracted to the puppy that is the first to approach them, but so much depends on which puppy had just been sleeping or which one had been playing hard just before someone arrives to see them.

With regard to physical characteristics, don't forget that these will alter with age and growth. The smallest puppy in the litter may turn out to be the biggest adult, for instance. Puppies invariably carry their tails up, sometimes over the back, but frequently the highest carried tail will be carried correctly at maturity. Also, always check the bite of your selected puppy to be sure that it is neither overshot or undershot. If you have a definite preference, though, amongst the puppies available, discuss this

DID YOU KNOW?
Your selection of a good puppy can be determined by your needs. A show potential or a good pet? It is your choice. Every puppy, however, should be of good temperament. Although show-quality puppies are bred and raised with emphasis on physical conformation, responsible breeders strive for equally good temperament. Do not buy from a breeder who concentrates solely on physical beauty at the expense of personality.

DID YOU KNOW?
You should not even think about buying a puppy that looks sick, undernourished, overly frightened or nervous. Sometimes a timid puppy will warm up to you after a 30-minute 'let's-get-acquainted' session.

specific puppy with the breeder and get his opinion.

You will normally be provided with a full diet sheet, worming history, information on insurance, pedigree, documentation on registration and an after-sales service. Most breeders would far prefer you to contact them with any worries or questions and will also be happy for you to return with the puppy for grooming advice as it grows.

WHERE TO BEGIN?
If you are convinced that the Bearded Collie is the ideal dog for you, it's time learn about where to find a puppy and what to look for. Locating a litter of Bearded Collies should not present a problem for the new owner. You should enquire about breeders in your area who enjoy a good reputation in the breed. You are looking for an established breeder with outstanding dog ethics and a strong commitment to the breed. New owners should have as many questions as they have doubts. An

You should select a puppy with clear, bright eyes, showing no discharge.

established breeder is indeed the one to answer your four million questions and make you comfortable with your choice of the Bearded Collie. An established breeder will sell you a puppy at a fair price if, and only if, the breeder determines that you are a suitable, worthy owner of his dogs. An established breeder can be relied upon for advice, no matter what time of day or night. A reputable breeder will accept a puppy back, without questions, should you decide that this not the right dog for you.

When choosing a breeder, reputation is much more important than convenience of location. Do not be overly impressed by breeders who run brag advertisements in the presses about their stupendous champions and working lines. The real quality breeders are quiet

DID YOU KNOW?

Your puppy should have a well-fed appearance but not a distended abdomen, which may indicate worms or incorrect feeding, or both. The body should be firm, with a solid feel. The skin of the abdomen should be pale pink and clean, without signs of scratching or rash. Check the hind legs to make certain that dewclaws were removed, if any were present at birth.

and unassuming. You hear about them at dog shows and by word of mouth. You may be well advised to avoid the novice who lives only a couple miles away. The local novice breeder, trying so hard to get rid of that first litter of puppies, is more than accommodating and anxious to sell you one. That breeder will charge you

DOCUMENTATION

Two important documents you will get from the breeder are the pup's pedigree and registration papers. The breeder should register the litter and each pup with The Kennel Club, and it is necessary for you to have the paperwork if you plan on showing or breeding in the future.

Make sure you know the breeder's intentions on which type of registration he will obtain for the pup. There are limited registrations which may prohibit the dog from being shown or from competing in non-conformation trials such as Working or Agility if the breeder feels that the pup is not of sufficient quality to do so. There is also a type of registration that will permit the dog in non-conformation competition only.

as much as any established breeder, but the novice breeder isn't going to interrogate you and your family about your intentions with the puppy, the environment

DID YOU KNOW?

Breeders rarely release puppies until they are eight to ten weeks of age. This is an acceptable age for most breeds of dog, excepting toy breeds, which are not released until around 12 weeks, given their petite sizes. If a breeder has a puppy that is 12 weeks or more, it is likely well socialised and housetrained. Be sure that it is otherwise healthy before deciding to take it home.

and training you can provide, etc. That breeder will be nowhere to be found when your poorly bred, badly adjusted four-pawed monster starts to growl and spit up at midnight or eat the family cat!

Whilst health considerations in the Bearded Collie are not nearly as daunting as in many other breeds, socialisation is a breeder concern of immense importance. Since the Bearded Collie's temperament can vary from line to line, socialisation is the first and best way to encourage a proper, stable personality.

Choosing a breeder is an important first step in dog ownership. Fortunately, the majority of Bearded Collie breeders are devoted to the breed and its well being. New owners should have little problem finding a reputable breeder who doesn't live on the other side of the country (or in a different country). The Kennel Club is able to recommend breeders of quality Bearded Collies, as can any local all-breed club or Bearded Collie club. Potential owners are encouraged to go to dog shows to see Bearded Collies in action, to meet the handlers firsthand and to get an idea of what Bearded Collies look like outside a photographer's lens. Provided you approach the handlers when they are not terribly busy with the dogs, most are more than willing to answer questions, recommend breeders and give advice.

INSURANCE
Many good breeders will offer you insurance with your new puppy, which is an excellent idea. The first few weeks of insurance will probably be covered free of charge or with only minimal cost, allowing you to take up the policy when this expires. If you own a pet dog, it is sensible to take out such a policy as veterinary fees can be high, although routine vaccinations and boosters are not covered. Look carefully at the many options open to you before deciding which suits you best.

It would be hard to select just one puppy from this adorable bunch. Choose the one that chooses you!

ARE YOU A FIT OWNER?

If the breeder from whom you are buying a puppy asks you a lot of personal questions, do not be insulted. Such a breeder wants to be sure that you will be a fit provider for his puppy.

Now that you have contacted and met a breeder or two and made your choice about which breeder is best suited to your needs, it's time to visit the litter. Keep in mind that many top breeders have waiting lists. Sometimes new owners have to wait as long as two years for a puppy. If you are really committed to the breeder whom you've selected, then you will wait (and hope for an early arrival!). If not, you may have to resort to your second or third choice breeder. Don't be too anxious, however. If the breeder doesn't have any waiting list, or any customers, there is probably a good reason. It's no different than visiting a pub with no clientele. The better pubs and restaurants always have a waiting list—and it's usually worth the wait.

The physical characteristics of the Bearded Collie will change with age. The smallest pup in the litter could turn out to be the largest adult. And coat colour will change also as a puppy grows.

Besides, isn't a puppy more important than a pint?

Since you are likely to be choosing a Bearded Collie as a pet dog and not a working dog, you simply should select a pup that is friendly and attractive. While the basic structure of the breed has little variation, the temperament may differ slightly in certain strains. Beware of the shy or overly aggressive puppy, and be especially conscious of the nervous Bearded Collie pup. Don't let sentiment or emotion trap you

YOUR SCHEDULE . . .

If you lead an erratic, unpredictable life, with daily or weekly changes in your work requirements, consider the problems of owning a puppy. The new puppy has to be fed regularly, socialised (loved, petted, handled, introduced to other people) and, most importantly, allowed to visit outdoors for toilet training. As the dog gets older, it can be more tolerant of deviations in its feeding and toilet relief.

Bring the whole family along when choosing a Bearded Collie. Children like to feel a part of the decision-making process.

43

The first order of business once you bring your new Bearded Collie home is to acclimate him to his crate. Never use the crate as a place of punishment.

into buying the runt of the litter.

If you have intentions of your new charge herding sheep, there are many more considerations. The parents of a future working dog should have excellent qualifications, including actual work experience as well as working titles in their pedigrees.

The gender of your puppy is largely a matter of personal taste, although there is a common belief amongst those who work with Bearded Collies that bitches are quicker to learn and generally more loving and faithful. Males learn more slowly but retain the lesson longer.

Breeders commonly allow visitors to see the litter by around the fifth or sixth week, and puppies leave for their new homes between the eighth and tenth week. Breeders who permit their puppies to leave early are more interested in your pounds than in their puppies' well-being. Puppies need to learn the rules of the trade from their dams, and most dams

continue teaching the pups manners and dos and don'ts until around the eighth week. Breeders spend significant amounts of time with the Bearded Collie toddlers so that they are able to interact with the 'other species,' i.e. humans. Given the long history that dogs and humans have, bonding between the two species is natural but must be nurtured. A well-bred, well-socialised Bearded Collie pup wants nothing more than to be near you and please you.

DID YOU KNOW?

The cost of food must also be mentioned. All dogs need a good quality food with an adequate supply of protein to develop their bones and muscles properly. Most dogs are not picky eaters but unless fed properly they can quickly succumb to skin problems.

COMMITMENT OF OWNERSHIP

After considering all of these factors, you have most likely already made some very important decisions about selecting your puppy. You have chosen a Bearded Collie, which means that you have decided which characteristics you want in a dog and what type of dog will best fit into your family and lifestyle. If you have selected a breeder, you have gone a step further—you have done your research and found a responsible, conscientious person who breeds quality Bearded Collies and who should be a reliable source of help as you and your puppy adjust to life together. If you have observed a litter in action, you have obtained a firsthand look at the dynamics of a puppy 'pack' and, thus, you should learn about each pup's individual personality—perhaps you have even found one that particularly appeals to you.

However, even if you have not yet found the Bearded Collie puppy of your dreams, observing pups will help you learn to recognise certain behaviour and to determine what a pup's behaviour indicates about his temperament. You will be able to pick out which pups are the leaders, which ones are less outgoing, which ones are confident, which ones are shy, playful, friendly, aggressive, etc. Equally as important, you will learn to recognise what a healthy pup should look and act like. All of these things will help you in your search, and when you

If you are choosing a Bearded Collie solely as a pet, simply choose one that is friendly and attractive. Your new pet should be attentive and energetic, though hopefully not hyperactive or uncontrollable.

find the Bearded Collie that was meant for you, you will know it!

Researching your breed, selecting a responsible breeder and observing as many pups as possible are all important steps on the way to dog ownership. It may seem like a lot of effort…and you have not even brought the pup home yet! Remember, though, you cannot be too careful when it comes to deciding on the type of dog you want and finding out about your prospective pup's background. Buying a puppy is not—or should not be—just another whimsical purchase. This is one instance in which you

Toys are a must for curious playful puppies, especially Bearded Collie puppies. Stimulate your puppy with a variety of toys to keep his mind busy and to limit his mischief-making.

actually do get to choose your own family! You may be thinking that buying a puppy should be fun—it should not be so serious and so much work. Keep in mind that your puppy is not a cuddly stuffed toy or decorative lawn

ornament, but a creature that will become a real member of your family. You will come to realise that, whilst buying a puppy is a pleasurable and exciting endeavour, it is not something to be taken lightly. Relax…the fun will start when the pup comes home!

Always keep in mind that a puppy is nothing more than a baby in a furry disguise…a baby who is virtually helpless in a human world and who trusts his owner for fulfilment of his basic needs for survival. In addition to water and shelter, your pup needs care, protection, guidance and love. If you are not prepared to commit to this, then you are not prepared to own a dog.

Wait a minute, you say. How hard could this be? All of my neighbours own dogs and they seem to be doing just fine. Why should I have to worry about all of this? Well, you should not worry about it; in fact, you will probably find that once your Bearded Collie pup gets used to his new home, he will fall into his place in the family quite naturally. But it never hurts to emphasise the commitment of dog ownership. With some time and patience, it is really not too difficult to raise a curious and exuberant Bearded Collie pup to be a well-adjusted and well-mannered adult dog—a dog that could be your most loyal friend.

PREPARING PUPPY'S PLACE IN YOUR HOME

Researching your breed and finding a breeder are only two aspects of the 'homework' you will have to do before bringing your Bearded Collie puppy home. You will also have to prepare your home and family for the new addition. Much as you would prepare a nursery for a newborn baby, you will need to designate a place in your home that will be the puppy's own. How you prepare your home will depend on how much freedom the dog will be allowed. Whatever you decide, you must ensure that he has a place that he can 'call his own.'

When you bring your new puppy into your home, you are bringing him into what will become his home as well. Obviously, you did not buy a puppy so that he could take over your house, but in order for a puppy to grow into a stable, well-adjusted dog, he has to feel comfortable in his surroundings. Remember, he is leaving the warmth and security of his mother and littermates, as well as the familiarity of the only place he has ever known, so it is important to make his transition as easy as possible. By preparing a place in your home for the puppy, you are making him feel as welcome as possible in a strange new place. It should not take him

long to get used to it, but the sudden shock of being transplanted is somewhat traumatic for a young pup. Imagine how a small child would feel in the same situation—that is how your puppy must be feeling. It is up to you to reassure him and to let him know, 'Little chap, you are going to like it here!'

When your Beardie pup first arrives home he will want to sniff out every new thing he comes across. This is how he gets acquainted with his new surroundings.

WHAT YOU SHOULD BUY

CRATE

To someone unfamiliar with the use of crates in dog training, it may seem like punishment to shut a dog in a crate, but this is not the case at all. Although all breeders do not advocate crate training, more and more breeders and trainers are recommending crates as a preferred tool for show puppies as well as pet puppies. Crates are not cruel—crates have

Pet shops sell quality crates that are soundly constructed and affordably priced. Purchase a medium-sized crate for the Beardie.

PHOTO COURTESY OF DISKOOIL.

inside, a crate becomes a cosy pseudo-den for your dog. Like his ancestors, he too will seek out the comfort and retreat of a den—you just happen to be providing him with something a little more luxurious than his early ancestors enjoyed.

As far as purchasing a crate, the type that you buy is up to you. It will most likely be one of the two most popular types: wire or fibreglass. There are advantages and disadvantages to each type. For example, a wire crate is more open, allowing the air to flow through and affording the dog a view of what is going on around him whilst a fibreglass crate is sturdier. Both can double as travel crates, providing protection for the dog. The size of the crate is another thing to consider. Puppies do not stay puppies forever—in fact, sometimes it seems as if they grow right before your eyes. A small crate may be fine for a very young Bearded Collie pup, but it will not do him much good for long! Unless you have the money and the inclination to buy a new crate every time your pup has a growth spurt, it is better to get one that will accommodate your dog both as a pup and at full size. A medium-size crate will be necessary for a full-grown Bearded Collie, who stands approximately 22 inches high.

Specialised dog crates can be very worthwhile, for many humane and highly effective uses in dog care and training. For example, crate training is a very popular and very successful housebreaking method. A crate can keep your dog safe during travel and, perhaps most importantly, a crate provides your dog with a place of his own in your home. It serves as a 'doggie bedroom' of sorts—your Bearded Collie can curl up in his crate when he wants to sleep or when he just needs a break. Many dogs sleep in their crates overnight. When lined with soft bedding and with a favourite toy intermittent use. The temperament of a Bearded Collie, being that it is a bouncy, sociable dog, does not lend itself to long periods of confinement. Therefore, periods spent in the dog crate should always be short, so that the dog sees the crate as a place of relaxation and not of restriction. Puppies, and adult dogs as well, should never be left in a crate needing to relieve themselves, as it is not suitable for a dog to be expected to stay in a crate 'holding on' to a full bladder.

CRATE TRAINING TIPS

During crate training, you should partition off the section of the crate in which the pup stays. If he is given too big an area, this will hinder your training efforts. Crate training is based on the fact that a dog does not like to soil his sleeping quarters, so it is ineffective to keep a pup in a crate that is so big that he can eliminate in one end and get far enough away from it to sleep. Also, you want to make the crate den-like for the pup. Blankets and a favourite toy will make the crate cosy for the small pup; as he grows, you may want to evict some of his 'roommates' to make more room.

It will take some coaxing at first, but be patient. Given some time to get used to it, your pup will adapt to his new home-within-a-home quite nicely.

Although your Beardie pup may not like it at first, with proper training he will come to think of his crate as his 'den.' Furnish it with a comfy blanket and a favourite toy.

BEDDING

Veterinary bedding in the dog's crate will help the dog feel more at home and you may also like to pop in a small blanket. This will take the place of the leaves, twigs, etc., that the pup would use in the wild to make a den; the pup can make his own 'burrow' in the crate. Although your pup is far removed from his den-making ancestors, the denning instinct is still a part of his genetic makeup. Second, until you bring your pup home, he has been sleeping amidst the warmth of his mother and littermates, and whilst a blanket is not the same as a warm,

Choose safe and durable toys for your Bearded Collie puppy. Visit the pet shop to see the wide selection.

TOYS, TOYS, TOYS!

With a big variety of dog toys available, and so many that look like they would be a lot of fun for a dog, be careful in your selection. It is amazing what a set of puppy teeth can do to an innocent-looking toy, so, obviously, safety is a major consideration. Be sure to choose the most durable products that you can find. Hard nylon bones and toys are a safe bet, and many of them are offered in different scents and flavours that will be sure to capture your dog's attention. It is always fun to play a game of catch with your dog, and there are balls and flying discs that are specially made to withstand dog teeth.

breathing body, it still provides heat and something with which to snuggle. You will want to wash your pup's bedding frequently in case he has an accident in his crate, and replace or remove any blanket that becomes ragged and starts to fall apart.

Toys

Toys are a must for dogs of all ages, especially for curious playful pups. Puppies are the 'children' of the dog world, and what child does not love toys? Chew toys provide enjoyment to both dog and owner—your dog will enjoy playing with his favourite toys, whilst you will enjoy the fact that they distract him from your expensive shoes and leather sofa. Puppies love to chew; in fact, chewing is a physical need for pups as they are teething, and everything looks appetising! The full range of your possessions—from old tea towel to Oriental carpet—are fair game in the eyes of a teething pup. Puppies are not all that discerning when it comes to finding something to literally 'sink their teeth into'—everything tastes great!

Bearded Collie puppies are fairly aggressive chewers and only the hardest, strongest toys should be offered to them. Breeders advise owners to resist stuffed toys, because they can become de-stuffed in no time. The overly excited pup may ingest the stuffing, which is neither digestible nor nutritious.

Similarly, squeaky toys are quite popular, but must be avoided for the Bearded Collie. Perhaps a squeaky toy can be used as an aid in training, but not for free play. If a pup 'disembowels' one of these, the small plastic squeaker inside can be dangerous if swallowed. Monitor the condition of all your pup's toys carefully and get rid of any that have been chewed to the point of becoming potentially dangerous.

Be careful of natural bones, which have a tendency to splinter into sharp, dangerous pieces. Also be careful of rawhide, which can turn into pieces that are easy to

swallow or into a mushy mess on your carpet.

LEAD

A nylon lead is probably the best option as it is the most resistant to puppy teeth should your pup take a liking to chewing on his lead. Of course, this is a habit that should be nipped in the bud, but if your pup likes to chew on his lead he has a very slim chance of being able to chew through the strong nylon. Nylon leads are also lightweight, which is good for a young Bearded Collie who is just getting used to the idea of walking on a lead. For everyday walking and safety purposes, the nylon lead is a good choice. As your pup grows up and gets used to walking on the lead, you may want to purchase a flexible lead. These leads allow you to extend the length to give the dog a

Bearded Collie pups are aggressive chewers. Stuffed toys probably should be avoided, as they can become de-stuffed in no time. Always supervise your pup carefully when presenting a new toy.

These are some items you will need to purchase for your new puppy. A buckle collar is needed to attach identification tags, and a nylon lead is best for walking your new Bearded Collie.

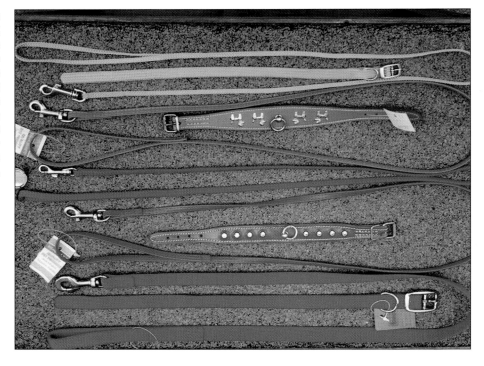

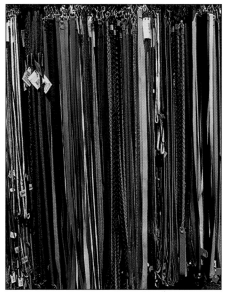

broader area to explore or to shorten the length to keep the dog close to you. Of course there are special leads for training purposes and for working Bearded Collies, but these are not necessary for routine walks.

COLLAR

Your pup should get used to wearing a collar all the time since you will want to attach his ID tags to it, and, of course, you have to attach the lead to something! A lightweight nylon collar is a good choice; make sure that it fits snugly enough so that the pup cannot wriggle out of it, but is

Choose the Right Collar for Your Dog

The BUCKLE COLLAR is the standard collar used for everyday purpose. Be sure that you adjust the buckle on growing puppies. Check it every day. It can become too tight overnight! These collars can be made of leather or nylon. Attach your dog's identification tags to this collar.

Buckle Collar

The CHOKE CHAIN is the usual collar recommended for training. It is constructed of highly polished steel so that it slides easily through the stainless steel loop. The idea is that the dog controls the pressure around its neck and he will stop pulling if the collar becomes uncomfortable. Never leave a choke collar on your dog when not training.

Choke Collar

The HALTER is for a trained dog that has to be restrained to prevent running away, chasing a cat and the like. Considered the most humane of all collars, it is frequently used on smaller dogs for which collars are not comfortable.

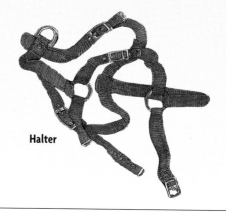

Halter

53

A veritable bowl of bowls can be found at your pet shop. Purchase two or four, depending on your circumstances.

A veritable bowl of bowls can be found at your pet shop. Purchase two or four, depending on your circumstances.

loose enough so that it will not be uncomfortably tight around the pup's neck. You should be able to fit a finger between the pup and the collar. It may take some time for your pup to get used to wearing the collar, but soon he will not even notice that it is there. Choke collars are made for training, but should only be used by an experienced handler.

FOOD AND WATER BOWLS

Your pup will need two bowls, one for food and one for water. You may want two sets of bowls, one for inside and one for outside, depending on where the dog will be fed and where he will be spending most of his time. Stainless steel or sturdy plastic bowls are popular choices. Plastic

FINANCIAL RESPONSIBILITY
Grooming tools, collars, leashes, dog beds and, of course, toys will be an expense to you when you first obtain your pup, and the cost will continue throughout your dog's lifetime. If your puppy damages or destroys your possessions (as most puppies surely will!) or something belonging to a neighbour, you can calculate additional expense. There is also flea and pest control, which every dog owner faces more than once. You must be able to handle the financial responsibility of owning a dog.

It is your responsibility to clean up after your dog has relieved himself. Pet shops have various aids to assist in the clean-up job.

bowls are more chewable. Dogs tend not to chew on the steel variety, which can be sterilised. It is important to buy sturdy bowls since anything is in danger of being chewed by puppy teeth and

better. All you can do is be prepared to clean up any 'accidents.' Old rags, towels, newspapers and a safe disinfectant are good to have on hand.

Steel bowls are more durable than plastic bowls and can be sterilised.

you do not want your dog to be constantly chewing apart his bowl (for his safety and for your purse!).

CLEANING SUPPLIES

Until a pup is housetrained you will be doing a lot of cleaning. Accidents will occur, which is okay in the beginning because the puppy does not know any

PUPPY-PROOFING

Thoroughly puppy-proof your house before bringing your puppy home. Never use roach or rodent poisons in any area accessible to the puppy. Avoid the use of toilet bowl cleaners. Most dogs are born with toilet bowl sonar and will take a drink if the lid is left open. Also keep the rubbish secured and out of reach.

55

NATURAL TOXINS

Examine your grass and garden landscaping before bringing your puppy home. Many varieties of plants have leaves, stems or flowers that are toxic if ingested, and you can depend on a curious puppy to investigate them. Ask your veterinarian for information on poisonous plants or research them at your library.

The items previously discussed are the bare necessities. You will find out what else you need as you go along—grooming supplies, flea/tick protection, baby gates to partition a room, etc. These things will vary depending on your situation but it is important that you have everything you need to feed and make your Bearded Collie comfortable in his first few days at home.

Even though your Beardie puppy may love the garden, his bed should be placed inside the home near the family's main living space.

PUPPY-PROOFING YOUR HOME

Aside from making sure that your Bearded Collie will be comfortable in your home, you also have to make sure that your home is safe for your Bearded Collie. This means taking precautions that your pup will not get into anything he should not get into and that there is nothing within his reach that may harm him should he sniff it, chew it, inspect it, etc. This probably seems obvious since, whilst you are primarily concerned with your pup's safety, at the same time you do not want your belongings to be ruined. Breakables should be placed out of reach if your dog is to have full run of the house. If he is to be limited to certain places within the house, keep any potentially dangerous items in the 'off-limits' areas. An electrical cord can pose a danger should the puppy decide to taste it—and who is going to convince a pup that it would not make a great chew toy? Cords should be fastened tightly against the wall. If your dog is going to spend time in a crate, make sure that there is nothing near his crate that he can reach if he sticks his curious little nose or paws through the openings. Just as you would with a child, keep all household cleaners and chemicals where the pup cannot get to them.

It is also important to make sure that the outside of your home

is safe. Of course your puppy should never be unsupervised, but a pup let loose in the garden will want to run and explore, and he should be granted that freedom. Do not let a fence give you a false sense of security; you would be surprised how crafty (and persistent) a dog can be in working out how to dig under and squeeze his way through small holes, or to jump or climb over a fence. The remedy is to make the fence high enough so that it really is impossible for your dog to get over it (about 3 metres should suffice), and well embedded into the ground. Be sure to repair or secure any gaps in the fence. Check the fence periodically to ensure that it is in good shape and make repairs as needed; a very

57

determined pup may return to the same spot to 'work on it' until he is able to get through.

FIRST TRIP TO THE VET

You have picked out your puppy, and your home and family are ready. Now all you have to do is collect your Bearded Collie from the breeder and the fun begins, right? Well…not so fast. Something else you need to prepare is your pup's first trip to the veterinary surgeon. Perhaps the breeder can recommend someone in the area that specialises in Bearded Collies, or maybe you know some other Bearded Collie owners who can suggest a good vet. Either way, you should have an appointment arranged for your pup before you pick him up and plan on taking

him for an examination before bringing him home.

The pup's first visit will consist of an overall examination to make sure that the pup does not have any problems that are not apparent to the eye. The veterinary surgeon will also set up a schedule for the pup's vaccinations; the breeder will inform you of which ones the pup has already received and the vet can continue from there.

INTRODUCTION TO THE FAMILY

Everyone in the house will be excited about the puppy's arrival and will want to pet him and play with him, but it is best to make the introduction low-key so as not to overwhelm the puppy. He is apprehensive already. It is the first

DID YOU KNOW?
You will probably start feeding your pup the same food that he has been getting from the breeder; the breeder should give you a few days' supply to start you off. Although you should not give your pup too many treats, you will want to have puppy treats on hand for coaxing, training, rewards, etc. Be careful, though, as a small pup's calorie requirements are relatively low and a few treats can add up to almost a full day's worth of calories without the required nutrition.

time he has been separated from his mother and the breeder, and the ride to your home is likely to be the first time he has been in a car. The last thing you want to do is smother him, as this will only frighten him further. This is not to say that human contact is not extremely necessary at this stage, because this is the time when a connection between the pup and

while. Gradually, each person should spend some time with the pup, one at a time, crouching down to get as close to the pup's level as possible and letting him sniff their hands and petting him gently. He definitely needs human attention and he needs to be touched—this is how to form an immediate bond. Just remember that the pup is experiencing a lot

Along with humans, it is a good idea to introduce your Beardie to the family cat. Who says cats and dogs don't get along?

his human family is formed. Gentle petting and soothing words should help console him, as well as just putting him down and letting him explore on his own (under your watchful eye, of course).

The pup may approach the family members or may busy himself with exploring for a

DID YOU KNOW?
It will take at least two weeks for your puppy to become accustomed to his new surroundings. Give him lots of love, attention, handling, frequent opportunities to relieve himself, a diet he likes to eat and a place he can call his own.

of things for the first time, at the same time. There are new people, new noises, new smells, and new things to investigate: so be gentle, be affectionate, and be as comforting as you can be.

PUP'S FIRST NIGHT HOME

You have travelled home with your new charge safely in his crate. He's been to the vet for a thorough check-up; he's been weighed, his papers examined; perhaps he's even been vaccinated and wormed as well. He's met the family, licked the whole family, including the excited children and the less-than-happy cat. He's explored his area, his new bed, the garden and anywhere else he's been permitted. He's eaten his first meal at home and relieved himself in the proper place. He's heard lots of new sounds, smelled new friends and seen more of the outside world than ever before.

DID YOU KNOW?

Some experts in canine health advise that stress during a dog's early years of development can compromise and weaken his immune system and may trigger the potential for a shortened life expectancy. They emphasise the need for happy and stress-free growing-up years.

TRAINING TIP

Training your puppy takes much patience and can be frustrating at times, but you should see results from your efforts. If you have a puppy that seems untrainable, take him to a trainer or behaviourist. The dog may have a personality problem that requires the help of a professional, or perhaps you need help in learning how to train your dog.

That was just the first day! He's worn out and is ready for bed…or so you think!

It's puppy's first night and you are ready to say 'Good night'—keep in mind that this is puppy's first night ever to be sleeping alone. His dam and littermates are no longer at paw's length and he's a bit scared, cold and lonely. Be reassuring to your new family member. This is not the time to spoil him and give in to his inevitable whining.

Puppies whine. They whine to let the others know where they are and hopefully to get company out of it. Place your pup in his new bed or crate in his room and close the door. Mercifully, he may fall asleep without a peep. If the inevitable occurs, ignore the whining: he is fine. Be strong and keep his interest in mind. Do not allow

BOY OR GIRL?

An important consideration to be discussed is the sex of your puppy. For a family companion, a bitch may be the better choice, considering the female's inbred concern for all young creatures and her accompanying tolerance and patience. It is always advisable to spay a pet bitch, which may guarantee her a longer life.

your heart to become guilty and visit the pup. He will fall asleep.

Many breeders recommend placing a piece of bedding from his former home in his new bed so that he recognises the scent of his littermates. Others still advise placing a hot water bottle in his bed for warmth. This

latter may be a good idea provided the pup doesn't attempt to suckle—he'll get good and wet and may not fall asleep so fast.

Puppy's first night can be somewhat stressful for the pup and his new family. Remember that you are setting the tone of nighttime at your house. Unless you want to play with your pup every evening at 10 p.m., midnight and 2 a.m., don't initiate the habit. Your family will thank you, and so will your pup!

PREVENTING PUPPY PROBLEMS

SOCIALISATION

Now that you have done all of the preparatory work and have helped your pup get accustomed to his new home and family, it is about time for you to have some fun! Socialising your Bearded Collie

SOCIALISATION

Thorough socialisation includes not only meeting new people but also being introduced to new experiences such as riding in the auto, having his coat brushed, hearing the television, walking in a crowd—the list is endless. The more your pup experiences, and the more positive the experiences are, the less of a shock and the less scary it will be for your pup to encounter new things.

A wire crate is a good choice for your Bearded Collie, as it is convenient for travel and affords the dog a full view of everything going on around him.

pup gives you the opportunity to show off your new friend, and your pup gets to reap the benefits of being an adorable furry creature that people will want to pet and, in general, think is absolutely precious!

Besides getting to know his new family, your puppy should be exposed to other people, animals and situations, but of course he must not come into close contact with dogs you don't know well until his course of injections is fully complete. This will help him become well adjusted as he grows up and less prone to being timid or fearful of the new things he will encounter. Your pup's sociali-sation began at the breeder's but now it is your responsibility to continue it. The socialisation he receives up until the age of 12

weeks is the most critical, as this is the time when he forms his impressions of the outside world. Be especially careful during the eight-to-ten-week period, also known as the fear period. The interaction he receives during this time should be gentle and reassuring. Lack of socialisation can manifest itself in fear and aggression as the dog grows up. He needs lots of human contact, affection, handling and exposure to other animals.

Once your pup has received his necessary vaccinations, feel free to take him out and about (on his lead, of course). Walk him around the neighbourhood, take him on your daily errands, let people pet him, let him meet other dogs and pets, etc. Puppies do not have to try to make friends;

Your puppy's socialisation began with his litter mates. It is your responsibility to continue this process after you take your puppy home.

there will be no shortage of people who will want to introduce themselves. Just make sure that you carefully supervise each meeting. If the neighbourhood children want to say hello, for example, that is great—children and pups most often make great companions. Sometimes an excited child can unintentionally handle a pup too roughly, or an overzealous pup can playfully nip a little too hard. You want to make socialisation experiences positive ones. What a pup learns during this very formative stage will impact his attitude toward future encounters. You want your dog to be comfortable around everyone. A pup that has a bad experience with a child may grow up to be a dog that is shy around or aggressive toward children.

CONSISTENCY IN TRAINING

Dogs, being pack animals, naturally need a leader, or else they try to establish dominance in their packs. When you bring a dog into your family, the choice of who becomes the leader and who becomes the 'pack' is entirely up to you! Your pup's intuitive quest for dominance, coupled with the fact that it is nearly impossible to look at an adorable Bearded Collie pup, with his 'puppy-dog' eyes and his floppy ears, and not cave in, give the pup almost an unfair advantage in getting the upper

A fence is required to keep your dog confined to your garden. Make sure that the fence is high enough that your Beardie cannot jump over it and that any gaps are secured and/or repaired.

hand! A pup will definitely test the waters to see what he can and cannot do. Do not give in to those pleading eyes—stand your ground when it comes to disciplining the pup and make sure that all family members do the same. It will only confuse the pup when Mother tells him to get off the couch when he is used to sitting up there with Father to watch the nightly news. Avoid discrepancies by having all members of the household decide on the rules before the pup even comes home…and be consistent in enforcing them! Early training shapes the dog's personality, so you cannot be unclear in what you expect.

63

COMMON PUPPY PROBLEMS

The best way to prevent puppy problems is to be proactive in stopping an undesirable behaviour as soon as it starts. The old saying 'You can't teach an old dog new tricks' does not necessarily hold true, but it is true that it is much easier to discourage bad behaviour in a young developing pup than to wait until the pup's bad behaviour becomes the adult dog's bad habit. There are some problems that are especially prevalent in puppies as they develop.

NIPPING

As puppies start to teethe, they feel the need to sink their teeth into anything available...unfortunately that includes your fingers, arms, hair, and toes. You may find this behaviour cute for the first five seconds...until you feel just how sharp those puppy teeth are. This is something you want to discourage immediately and consistently with a firm 'No!' (or whatever number of firm 'No's' it takes for him to understand that you mean business). Then replace your finger with an appropriate chew toy. Whilst this behaviour is merely annoying when the dog is young, it can become dangerous as your Bearded Collie's adult teeth grow in and his jaws develop, and he continues to think it is okay to gnaw on human appendages. Your Bearded Collie does not mean any harm with a friendly nip, but he also does not know his own strength.

CRYING/WHINING

Your pup will often cry, whine, whimper, howl or make some

CHEWING TIPS

Chewing goes hand in hand with nipping in the sense that a teething puppy is always looking for a way to soothe his aching gums. In this case, instead of chewing on you, he may have taken a liking to your favourite shoe or something else which he should not be chewing. Again, realise that this is a normal canine behaviour that does not need to be discouraged, only redirected. Your pup just needs to be taught what is acceptable to chew on and what is off limits. Consistently tell him NO when you catch him chewing on something forbidden and give him a chew toy. Conversely, praise him when you catch him chewing on something appropriate. In this way you are discouraging the inappropriate behaviour and reinforcing the desired behaviour. The puppy chewing should stop after his adult teeth have come in, but an adult dog continues to chew for various reasons—perhaps because he is bored, perhaps to relieve tension or perhaps he just likes to chew. That is why it is important to redirect his chewing when he is still young.

type of commotion when he is left alone. This is basically his way of calling out for attention to make sure that you know he is there and that you have not forgotten about him. He feels insecure when he is left alone, when you are out of the house and he is in his crate or when you are in another part of the house and he cannot see you. The noise he is making is an expression of the anxiety he feels at being alone, so he needs to be taught that being alone is okay. You are not actually training the dog to stop making noise, you are training him to feel comfortable when he is alone and thus removing the need for him to make the noise. This is where the crate with cosy bedding and a toy comes in handy. You want to know that he is safe when you are not there to supervise, and you

The amount of water your puppy takes in should be carefully monitored.

know that he will be safe in his crate rather than roaming freely about the house. In order for the pup to stay in his crate without making a fuss, he needs to be comfortable in his crate. On that note, it is extremely important that the crate is never used as a form of punishment, or the pup will have a negative association with the crate.

Accustom the pup to the crate in short, gradually increasing time intervals in which you put him in the crate, maybe with a treat, and stay in the room with him. If he cries or makes a fuss, do not go to him, but stay in his sight. Gradually he will realise that staying in his crate is all right without your help, and it will not be so traumatic for him when you are not around. You may want to leave the radio on softly when you leave the house; the sound of human voices may be comforting to him.

DID YOU KNOW?

The majority of problems that is commonly seen in young pups will disappear as your dog gets older. However, how you deal with problems when he is young will determine how he reacts to discipline as an adult dog. It is important to establish who is boss (hopefully it will be you!) right away when you are first bonding with your dog. This bond will set the tone for the rest of your life together.

DIETARY AND FEEDING CONSIDERATIONS

Today the choices of food for your Bearded Collie are many and varied. There are simply dozens of brands of food in all sorts of flavours and textures, ranging from puppy diets to those for seniors. There are even hypoallergenic and low-calorie diets available. Because your Bearded Collie's food has a bearing on coat, health and temperament, it is essential that the most suitable diet is selected for a Bearded Collie of his age. It is fair to say, however, that even dedicated owners can be somewhat perplexed by the enormous range of foods available. Only understanding what is best for your dog will help you reach a valued decision.

DID YOU KNOW?
A good test for proper diet is the colour, odour, and firmness of your dog's stool. A healthy dog usually produces three semi-hard stools per day. The stools should have no unpleasant odour. They should be the same colour from excretion to excretion.

Dog foods are produced in three basic types: dried, semi-moist and tinned. Dried foods are useful for the cost-conscious for overall they tend to be less expensive than semi-moist or tinned. These contain the least fat and the most preservatives. Whilst

DID YOU KNOW?
You must store your dried dog food carefully. Open packages of dog food quickly lose their vitamin value, usually within 90 days of being opened. Mould spores and vermin could also contaminate the food.

flake-maize-type all-in-one meals are suitable for a lot of dogs, some will find them indigestible and are better on the expanded dried foods. Always feed the dried all-in-one foods soaked as per manufacturer's recommendations. In general tinned foods are made up of 60–70 percent water, whilst semi-moist ones often contain so much sugar that they are perhaps the least preferred by owners, even though their dogs seem to like them. With any diet, it is essential to provide plenty of fresh drinking water.

When selecting your dog's diet, three stages of development must be considered: the puppy stage, adult stage and the senior or veteran stage.

PUPPY STAGE

Puppies instinctively want to suck milk from their mother's teats and a normal puppy will exhibit this

Milk from their mother provides these Bearded Collie puppies with colostrum, which protects the puppies during their first ten weeks of life.

FOOD PREFERENCE

Selecting the best dried dog food is difficult. There is no majority consensus amongst veterinary scientists as to the value of nutrient analyses (protein, fat, fibre, moisture, ash, cholesterol, minerals, etc.). All agree that feeding trials are what matters, but you also have to consider the individual dog. Its weight, age, activity and what pleases its taste, all must be considered. It is probably best to take the advice of your veterinary surgeon. Every dog's dietary requirements vary, even during the lifetime of a particular dog.

If your dog is fed a good dried food, it does not require supplements of meat or vegetables. Dogs do appreciate a little variety in their diets so you may choose to stay with the same brand, but vary the flavour. Alternatively you may wish to add a little flavoured stock to give a difference to the taste.

---

behaviour from just a few moments following birth. If puppies do not attempt to suckle within the first half-hour or so, they should be encouraged to do so by placing them on the nipples, having selected ones with plenty of milk. This early milk supply is important in providing colostrum to protect the puppies during the first eight to ten weeks of their lives. Although a mother's milk is much better than any milk formula, despite there being some excellent ones available, if the puppies do not feed, you will have to feed them yourself. For those with less experience, advice from a veterinary surgeon is important so that you feed not only the right quantity of milk but that of correct quality, fed at suitably frequent intervals, usually every two hours during the first few days of life. Puppies

67

diets are not suitable for young Beardies and should not be introduced until the puppy is at least seven to nine months of age and then only gradually. The frequency of meals will have been reduced over time, and only when a young dog has reached the age of 12 months or older should an adult diet be fed.

Puppy and junior diets should be well balanced for the needs of your dog, so that except in certain circumstances additional vitamins, minerals and proteins will not be required.

ADULT DIETS

A dog is considered an adult when it has stopped growing, so in general the diet of a Bearded Collie can be changed to an adult one at about 12 months of age. Again you should rely upon your veterinary surgeon or dietary

Your dog's dental health is directly related to his diet, as well as a regular cleaning regimen. As your Bearded Collie matures, his teeth will get stronger.

Consult your veterinary surgeon for an acceptable maintenance diet for your adult Bearded Collie. Dried foods should be offered according to the manufacturer's instructions.

should be allowed to nurse from their mothers for about the first six weeks, although from the third or fourth week you will have begun to introduce small portions of suitable solid food. Most breeders like to introduce alternate milk and meat meals initially, building up to weaning time.

By the time the puppies are seven or a maximum of eight weeks old, they should be fully weaned and fed solely on a proprietary puppy food. Selection of the most suitable, good-quality diet at this time is essential for a puppy's fastest growth rate is during the first year of life. Puppies should initially be fed according to the diet they received from the breeder, varying the food gradually as the puppy grows. When selecting an all-in-one diet specifically formulated for puppies, be guided by your veterinary surgeon. Flake-maize

specialist to recommend an acceptable maintenance diet. Major dog food manufacturers specialise in this type of food, and it is just necessary for you to select the one best suited to your dog's needs. Active dogs may have different requirements than sedate dogs.

I find that the majority of adult Beardies do not respond well being fed on a high-protein diet. Therefore, if choosing an all-in-one food for an adult, choose the lower protein (pet) variety and not one for breeding or working animals.

SENIOR DIETS

As dogs get older, their metabolism changes. The older dog usually exercises less, moves more slowly and sleeps more. This change in lifestyle and physiological performance requires a change in diet. Since these changes take place slowly, they might not be recognisable. What is easily recognisable is weight gain. By continuing to feed your dog an adult-maintenance diet when it is slowing down metabolically, your dog will gain weight. Obesity in an older dog compounds the health problems that already accompany old age.

As your dog gets older, few of their organs function up to par. The kidneys slow down and the intestines become less efficient. These age-related factors are best

GRAIN-BASED DIETS

Many adult diets are based on grain. There is nothing wrong with this as long as it does not contain soy meal. Diets based on soy often cause flatulence (passing gas).

Grain-based diets are almost always the least expensive and a good grain diet is just as good as the most expensive diet containing animal protein.

There are many cases, however, when your dog might require a special diet. These special requirements should only be recommended by your veterinary surgeon.

Offer your Beardie puppy a puppy diet until he is 12 months of age. Your breeder can advise you about her success with quality brands and varieties.

69

handled with a change in diet and a change in feeding schedule to give smaller portions that are more easily digested.

There is no single best diet for every older dog. Whilst many dogs do well on light or senior diets, other dogs do better on puppy diets or other special premium diets such as lamb and rice. Be sensitive to your senior Bearded Collie's diet and this will help control other problems that may arise with your old friend.

WATER

Just as your dog needs proper nutrition from his food, water is an essential 'nutrient' as well. Water keeps the dog's body properly hydrated and promotes

Water should always be made available to your Bearded Collie. Whenever you go on trips with your Bearded Collie, make sure to bring water with you.

normal function of the body's systems. Your Bearded Collie should have access to clean fresh water at all times. Keep the dog's water bowl clean and change the water often, making sure that water is always available for your dog, especially if you feed dried food.

EXERCISE

From my many years' experience, I feel that the absolute best and most natural exercise for Beardies is free running. This is a great deal more enjoyable for the dog than walking on a lead and usually much simpler for you. Really, I think, it is almost essential to have a large garden and/or immediate access to a field or other suitable area, if you own a Beardie. Bearded Collies are generally rather dependent on plenty of exercise for their health and sanity, and for that of their owners!

Puppies should be offered a level of free exercise appropriate to their age and development. Beardie puppies should be encouraged to take rest periods as they will sometimes overtire themselves, especially when running with another dog.

Exercising your adult dog with another dog is most enjoyable for the Beardie. Beardies generally get on well with other breeds, although their exuberance can sometimes

What are you feeding your dog?

Read the label on your dog food. Many dog foods only advise what 50—55% of the contents are, leaving the other 45% in doubt.

1.3% Calcium

1.6% Fatty Acids

4.6% Crude Fibre

11% Moisture

14% Crude Fat

22% Crude Protein

45.5% ? ? ?

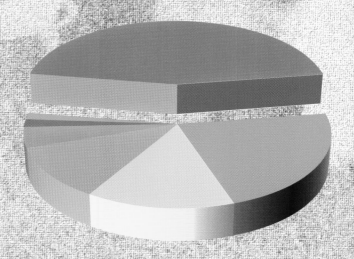

overpower a small or timid dog. It goes without saying that, although Beardies usually come when called, they should always run free in a safe area so they do not pose a nuisance or risk to themselves or others.

Bear in mind that an overweight dog should never be suddenly over-exercised; instead he should be allowed to increase exercise slowly. Not only is exercise essential to keep the dog's body fit, it is essential to his mental well-being. A bored dog will find something to do, which often manifests itself in some type of destructive behaviour. In this sense, it is essential for the owner's mental well-being as well!

GROOMING EQUIPMENT

How much grooming equipment you purchase will depend on how much grooming you are going to do. Here are some basics:

- Natural bristle brush
- Slicker brush
- Metal comb
- Metal pin brush
- Scissors
- Blaster
- Rubber mat
- Dog shampoo
- Spray hose attachment
- Ear cleaner
- Cotton wipes
- Towels
- Nail clippers

The Beardie is an exuberant dog who loves and needs exercise. This Bearded Collie is competing in an agility trial.

GROOMING

As far as long-coated breeds go, I find that Beardies have one of the easier coats to care for. However, they do get big coats and you should be very sure you want to have this constant consideration before you acquire a Beardie.

It is absolutely essential that you regularly groom your Beardie thoroughly from early puppyhood. This not only keeps the coat growing in a healthy way but also ensures that your puppy knows that grooming is a part of his life. You can put the puppy on your knee or stand it on a table with a suitable non-slip surface. Use a fairly soft brush and groom the puppy all over. This is not a time for play, so don't let your puppy chew or play with the brush. Likewise, no growling or snapping is allowed. It is very important to show the puppy that this is a serious business, thus reinforcing that your puppy grows up knowing that there is no way out of being a well-groomed dog! At the same time the experience should be a pleasurable one so always give plenty of praise and end with pats and cuddles.

If you are having grooming problems, always consult an expert: the breeder of your dog, another Beardie exhibitor or an experienced owner. Usually one of these professionals will be happy to try to help you and your dog.

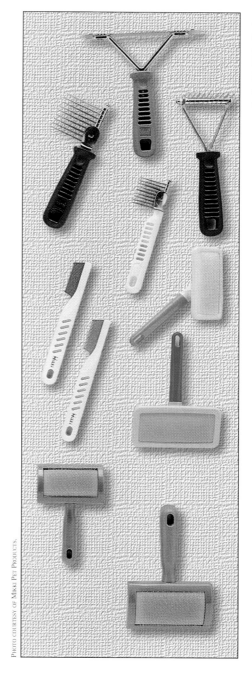

PHOTO COURTESY OF MIKKI PET PRODUCTS.

A wide array of grooming tools is available at your local pet shop. Purchase tools once: buy quality the first time.

BATHING AND BRUSHING

Contrary to popular belief, you can regularly bath your Beardie. Bathing will usually encourage the coat to maintain good condition, which in turn should make it easier to groom. Puppy coats respond well to bathing with puppy shampoos, but I would always use a conditioner after shampooing. Remember to rinse the coat very thoroughly. As with brushing, bathing is a serious business and your puppy should be encouraged to see it in this light. Puppies will often be apprehensive of the bath and should have plenty of reassurance. The Beardie should be expected to stand sensibly in the bath and resist a strong Beardie urge to bounce and play!

After bathing, towel-dry and ensure that your puppy becomes fully dry in a warm atmosphere. Always brush the coat whilst it is still damp. In this way, the coat retains resistance to knot and tangle formation.

Puppies should also expect to have their ears and eyes looked at during bathing and drying, so they are prepared for attention to these areas when they are adults.

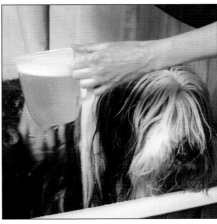

You can and should regularly bath your Bearded Collie to keep the coat in good condition. Be sure to thoroughly brush the coat through before beginning the bath. Keep soap out of your Beardie's eyes and water away from his ears.

As your Beardie's coat grows, it will alter in colour and texture. A fluffy undercoat will combine with a harsher, strong outer coat. Around six months or so, the first tangles and knots will start to appear, as if by magic. Behind the ears and between the legs will be prime targets, and the soft skin there makes it hard for a Beardie to accept the necessary grooming, at first. It is essential that you handle the dog appropriately at the stage of first removing knots. The dog must see that you are sympathetic but emphatic, as there is no room for the Beardie growling or snapping.

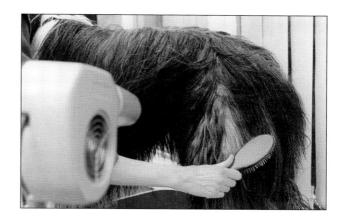

If you never intend to show your Beardie, you may decide to trim the hair behind the ears, on the tummy and between the front and hind legs. This can be done without outwardly spoiling the look of the coat at all. You may wish to have this done profession-ally, as there is a risk of cutting the delicate skin if not done with extreme care.

I find it best to continue to bath the coat on a fairly regular basis. You should always use a dog-specific shampoo and conditioning rinse for best results.

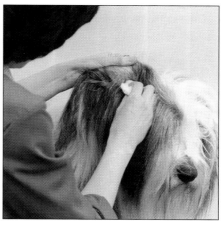

After the bath, a heavy-duty blaster (set on low) is ideal for drying the coat. During all grooming sessions, your Bearded Collie is expected to stand patiently for brushing, de-tangling and ear cleaning.

Your Bearded Collie puppy should become accustomed to grooming at a young age or else it will be troublesome to groom him when he gets older.

you wish your dog to lie down, you will need to train it to accept this from puppyhood, with love and reassurance.

MATS AND SPECIAL CONSIDERATIONS
Despite regular grooming, mats will sometimes occur. These should be removed by gently teasing them out with the fingers and thumbs. Tease from the lower edge of the knot or mat towards the skin, pulling the knot apart and ensuring that you do not pull at the dog's skin. Brushing every so often, as you tease the coat apart, will help to open the knot out. Specialist knot removers are

When grooming the longer Beardie coat, it is sensible to work systematically over the whole dog. Turn the coat so that the roots of the coat are exposed and brush from root to tip in long sweeping strokes with the lie of the coat. I prefer to use a metal pin brush with blunted metal tips on a pneumatic rubber base. A metal slicker brush can also be useful for knot removal; it should be used totally flat and with some caution, as it may cause soreness to the skin if not used correctly. A wide-toothed metal comb is useful for ensuring no small tangles remain at the end of a thorough grooming routine. I like to groom my dogs standing, but many people prefer them to lie down. If

available, which you might find useful. It is always necessary to completely groom the dog after any bathing routine. Any tangles left at this time will quickly escalate to difficult-to-manage mats in as short a time as a few days.

If you have left the dog's coat until he has a few mated areas, you should always groom the coat before bathing as the bathing process will 'set' the mats and make their removal painful to the dog. Obviously, it is far better to groom regularly and so prevent the bulkier tangles from forming.

The eyes of the Beardie

A pinbrush is effective in keeping the Beardie's coat tangle-free.

require special attention. Ideally there should not be a lot of coat growth around the eyes of the adult Beardie, but the young dog may have a fairly thick coat growth here. You can tie the coat up with a soft elastic hair ring, but this should be removed if the Beardie is not being directly supervised as the dog might remove the elastic and eat or choke on it.

Alternatively, you can trim above the eyes. This requires great care and is best done profession- ally, if you are at all in doubt as to your abilities. Once the coat is trimmed, it will probably require regular re-trimming as it will, initially, grow back thickly. However, if you leave the coat to

Brushing your Bearded Collie daily will help prevent tangles from forming. Most owners prefer to do this whilst the dog is standing or lying on a grooming table. The grooming table will make brushing your dog more comfortable for you and your dog.

The hair in your Beardie's ears will begin to grow as he gets older. You need to gently pluck this hair with your fingers or cankers may form.

mature naturally, it will grow and thin out with adulthood. Regularly check your dog's eyes for cleanliness and use cooled boiled water to bath them if necessary. Obviously any unusual discharge should be examined and treated by your veterinary surgeon.

Beardie coats do change and undergo moulting seasons. At these times the undercoat has an increased tendency to mat into the top coat and frequent grooming is essential. Bitches will invariably

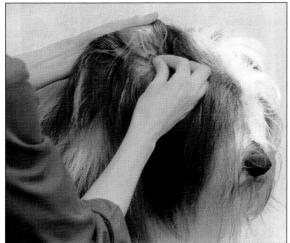

GROOMING TIP

Once you are sure that the dog is thoroughly rinsed, squeeze the excess water out of the coat with your hand and dry him with a heavy towel. You may choose to use a blaster on his coat or just let it dry naturally. In cold weather, never allow your dog outside with a wet coat.

There are 'dry bath' products on the market, which are sprays and powders intended for spot cleaning, that can be used between regular baths, if necessary. They are not substitutes for regular baths, but they are easy to use for touch-ups as they do not require rinsing.

lose a lot of coat around the time of and after their oestrus seasons. I find that my male Beardies tend to lose coat early in the year.

If you find that you really cannot cope with the dog's coat and you definitely know that you will never wish to show your dog, you can always resort to having the entire coat trimmed. This is a great pity as you will no longer have the naturally beautiful longer coat, but it is certainly preferable to a mated, unhappy dog and a guilt-ridden owner. In fact, Beardies absolutely love having their coats trimmed and feel free, airy and much younger. Trimming the coat will mean it is very hard to regain the full coat. Even though the Beardie's hair grows quickly, the full length will not be regained for two to three years, and then not without going through a hard-to-manage phase. Trimming should really be done professionally for best results. I would suggest that you ask for the dog to be trimmed and not clipped. Clipping the dog's coat will result in an ultra-short finish, which is, initially, rather unsightly and a bit of a shock to the dog in terms of comfort and draught proofing!

EAR CLEANING

As your Beardie matures, the hair in the ears will grow and need attention. Using the thumb and forefinger, pluck the hair gently from the ears. The hair in this area is very soft and comes away fairly easily. If you use a very light sprinkling of a veterinary-approved ear powder, the process is easier. There is some brief discomfort to the dog but, since leaving the hair in the ears promotes canker formation, removing the hair is preferable. After clearing the ear of hair and leaving the skin to settle, use an ear wipe with a veterinary-approved ear cleanser to remove waxy deposits. Be on the lookout for any signs of infection or ear mite infestation. If your Bearded Collie has been shaking his head or scratching at his ears frequently, this usually indicates a problem. Any discharge or unpleasant smell should be checked by your veterinary surgeon.

DID YOU KNOW?

The use of human soap products like shampoo, bubble bath and hand soap can be damaging to a dog's coat and skin. Human products are too strong and remove the protective oils coating the dog's hair and skin (making him water-resistant). Use only shampoo made especially for dogs and you may like to use a medicated shampoo, which will always help to keep external parasites at bay.

When you cut your Beardie's nails, hold the paw in one hand and take off the end of each nail in one quick clip.

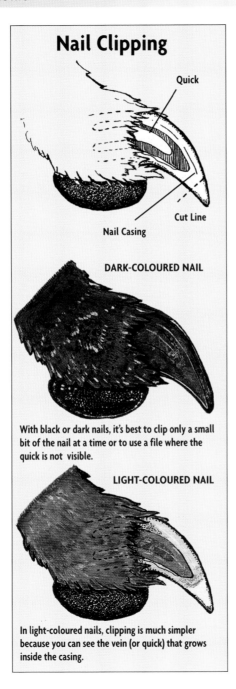

Nail Clipping

Quick

Cut Line

Nail Casing

DARK-COLOURED NAIL

With black or dark nails, it's best to clip only a small bit of the nail at a time or to use a file where the quick is not visible.

LIGHT-COLOURED NAIL

In light-coloured nails, clipping is much simpler because you can see the vein (or quick) that grows inside the casing.

NAIL CLIPPING

Your Bearded Collie should be accustomed to having his nails trimmed at an early age, since it will be part of your maintenance routine throughout his life. Not only does it look nicer, but long nails can scratch someone unintentionally. Also, a long nail has a better chance of ripping and bleeding, or causing the feet to spread. A good rule of thumb is that if you can hear your dog's nails clicking on the floor when he walks, his nails are too long.

Before you start cutting, make sure you can identify the 'quick' in each nail. The quick is a blood vessel that runs through the centre of each nail and grows rather close to the end. It will bleed if accidentally cut, which will be quite painful for the dog as it contains nerve endings. Keep some type of clotting agent on hand, such as a styptic pencil or styptic powder (the type used for shaving). This will stop the bleeding quickly when applied to the end of the cut nail. Do not panic if this happens, just stop the bleeding and talk soothingly to your dog. Once he has calmed down, move on to the next nail. It is better to clip a little at a time, particularly with black-nailed dogs.

Hold your pup steady as you begin trimming his nails; you do not want him to make any sudden movements or run away. Talk to him soothingly and stroke him as you clip. Holding his foot in your hand, simply take off the end of each nail in one quick clip. You can purchase nail clippers that are specially made for dogs; you can probably find them wherever you buy pet or grooming supplies.

TRAVELLING WITH YOUR DOG
CAR TRAVEL
You should accustom your Bearded Collie to riding in a car at an early age. You may or may not take him in the car often, but at the very least he will need to go to the vet and you do not want these trips to be traumatic for the dog or a big hassle for you. The safest way for a dog to ride in the car is in his crate. If he uses a crate in the house, you can use the same crate for travel.

Put the pup in the crate and see how he reacts. If he seems uneasy, you can have a passenger hold him on his lap whilst you drive. Another option is a

TRAVEL TIP
Never leave your dog alone in the car. In hot weather your dog can die from the high temperature inside a closed vehicle; even a car parked in the shade can heat up very quickly. Leaving the window open is dangerous as well since the dog can hurt himself trying to get out.

TRAVEL TIP
If you are going on a long motor trip with your dog, be sure the hotels are dog friendly. Many hotels do not accept dogs. Also take along some ice that can be thawed and offered to your dog if he becomes overheated. Most dogs like to lick ice.

specially made safety harness for dogs, which straps the dog in much like a seat belt. Do not let the dog roam loose in the vehicle—this is very dangerous! If you should stop short, your dog can be thrown and injured. If the dog starts climbing on you and pestering you whilst you are driving, you will not be able to concentrate on the road. It is an unsafe situation for everyone—human and canine.

For long trips, be prepared to stop to let the dog relieve himself. Bring along whatever you need to clean up after him. You should take along some paper kitchen towels and perhaps some old towelling for use should he have an accident in the car or suffer from travel sickness.

AIR TRAVEL
Whilst it is possible to take a dog on a flight within Britain, this is fairly unusual and advance permission is always required.

The dog will be required to travel in a fibreglass crate and you should always check in advance with the airline regarding specific requirements. To help the dog be at ease, put one of his favourite toys in the crate with him. Do not feed the dog for at least six hours before the trip to minimise his need to relieve himself. However, certain regulations specify that water must always be made available to the dog in the crate.

Make sure your dog is properly identified and that your contact information appears on his ID tags and on his crate. Animals travel in a different area

TRAVEL TIP

For international travel you will have to make arrangements well in advance (perhaps months), as countries' regulations pertaining to bringing in animals differ. There may be special health certificates and/or vaccinations that your dog will need before taking the trip, sometimes this has to be done within a certain time frame. In rabies-free countries, you will need to bring proof of the dog's rabies vaccination and there may be a quarantine period upon arrival.

The safest and most acceptable way of travelling with your Beardie is in a crate. Driving with a dog loose in a car is very dangerous. Your Bearded Collie should always be safe in his crate when travelling in the car.

of the plane than human passengers so every rule must be strictly adhered to so as to prevent the risk of getting separated from your dog.

BOARDING

So you want to take a family holiday—and you want to include all members of the family. You would probably make arrangements for accommodations ahead of time anyway, but this is especially important when travelling with a dog. You do not want to make an overnight stop at the only place around for miles and find out that they do not allow dogs. Also, you do not want to reserve a place for your family without confirming that you are travelling with a dog because if it is against their policy you may not have a place to stay.

Alternatively, if you are travelling and choose not to bring your Bearded Collie, you will have to make arrangements for him whilst you are away. Some options are to

take him to a neighbour's house to stay whilst you are gone, to have a trusted neighbour pop in often or stay at your house, or bring your dog to a reputable boarding kennel. If you choose to board him at a kennel, you should visit in advance to see the facilities provided, how clean they are and where the dogs are kept. Talk to some of the employees and see how they treat the dogs—do they spend time with the dogs, play with them, exercise them, etc.? Also find out the kennel's policy on vaccinations and what they

If you cannot take your dogs on holiday with you, it will be necessary to find a reputable boarding facility. Many Beardie folk cannot bear the thought of leaving their beloved chums and plan their holidays around their dogs!

TRAVEL TIP

When travelling, never let your dog off-lead in a strange area. Your dog could run away out of fear or decide to chase a passing squirrel or cat or simply want to stretch his legs without restriction—you might never see your canine friend again.

Locate a reputable boarding kennel before you actually need one.

require. This is for all of the dogs' safety, since when dogs are kept together, there is a greater risk of diseases being passed from dog to dog.

IDENTIFICATION

Your Bearded Collie is your valued companion and friend. That is why you always keep a close eye on him and you have made sure that he cannot escape from the garden or wriggle out of his collar and run away from you. However, accidents can happen and there may come a time when your

Your Beardie's ID tag should include your name, address and phone number.

IDENTIFICATION

If your dog gets lost, he is not able to ask for directions home.

Identification tags fastened to the collar give important information—the dog's name, the owner's name, the owner's address and a telephone number where the owner can be reached. This makes it easy for whom ever finds the dog to contact the owner and arrange to have the dog returned. An added advantage is that a person will be more likely to approach a lost dog who has ID tags on his collar; it tells the person that this is somebody's pet rather than a stray. This is the easiest and fastest method of identification provided that the tags stay on the collar and the collar stays on the dog.

dog unexpectedly gets separated from you. If this unfortunate event should occur, the first thing on your mind will be finding him. Proper identification, including an ID tag, a

As puppies become more and more expensive, especially those puppies of high quality for showing and/or breeding, they have a greater chance of being stolen. The usual collar dog tag is, of course, easily removed. But there are two techniques that have become widely used for identification.

The puppy microchip implantation involves the injection of a small microchip, about the size of a corn kernel, under the skin of the dog. If your dog shows up at a clinic or shelter, or is offered for resale under less than savory circumstances, it can be positively identified by the microchip. The microchip is scanned and a registry quickly identifies you as the owner. This is not only protection against theft, but should the dog run away or go chasing a squirrel and get lost, you have a fair chance of getting it back.

Tattooing is done on various parts of the dog, from its belly to its cheeks. The number tattooed can be your telephone number or any other number which you can easily memorise. When professional dog thieves see a tattooed dog, they usually lose interest in it. Both microchipping and tattooing can be done at your local veterinary clinic. For the safety of our dogs, no laboratory facility or dog broker will accept a tattooed dog as stock.

tattoo, and possibly a microchip, will increase the chances of his being returned to you safely and quickly.

It is not uncommon for a dog to roam and become lost from its owner. Therefore, it is important that your Bearded Collie is properly identified whether by tattoo, microchip and/or ID tags.

Living with an untrained dog is a lot like owning a piano that you do not know how to play—it is a nice object to look at but it does not do much more than that to bring you pleasure. Now try taking piano lessons and suddenly the piano comes alive and brings forth magical sounds and rhythms that set your heart singing and your body swaying.

The same is true with your Bearded Collie. Any dog is a big responsibility and if not trained sensibly may develop unacceptable behaviour that annoys you or could even cause family friction.

To train your Bearded Collie, you may like to enrol in an obedience class. Teach him good manners as you learn how and why he behaves the way he does. Find out how to communicate with your dog and how to recognise and understand his communications with you. Suddenly the dog takes on a new role in your life—he is clever, interesting, well behaved and fun to be with. He demonstrates his bond of devotion to you daily. In other words, your Bearded Collie does wonders for your ego because he constantly reminds you that you are not only his leader, you are his hero!

Those involved with teaching dog obedience and counselling owners about their dogs' behaviour have discovered some interesting facts about dog ownership. For example, training dogs when they are puppies results in the highest rate of success in developing well-mannered and well-adjusted adult dogs. Training an older dog, from six months to six years of age, can produce almost equal results providing that the owner accepts the dog's slower rate of learning capability and is willing to work patiently to help the dog succeed at developing to his fullest potential. Unfortunately,

PATIENCE . . .
If you start with a normal, healthy dog and give him time, patience and some carefully executed lessons, you will reap the rewards of that training for the life of the dog. And what a life it will be! The two of you will find immeasurable pleasure in the companionship you have built together with love, respect and understanding.

86

DID YOU KNOW?

To a dog's way of thinking, your hands are like his mouth in terms of a defence mechanism. If you squeeze him too tightly, he might just bite you because that would be his normal response. This is not aggressive biting and, although all biting should be discouraged, you need the discipline in learning how to handle your dog.

many owners of untrained adult dogs lack the patience factor, so they do not persist until their dogs are successful at learning particular behaviours.

Training a puppy aged 10 to 16 weeks (20 weeks at the most) is like working with a dry sponge in a pool of water. The pup soaks up whatever you show him and constantly looks for more things to do and learn. At this early age, his body is not yet producing hormones, and therein lies the reason for such a high rate of success. Without hormones, he is focused on his owners and not particularly interested in investi-gating other places, dogs, people, etc. You are his leader: his provider of food, water, shelter and security. He latches onto you and wants to stay close. He will usually follow you from room to room, will not let you out of his sight when you are outdoors

with him, and will respond in like manner to the people and animals you encounter. If you greet a friend warmly, he will be happy to greet the person as well. If, however, you are hesitant, even anxious, about the approach of a stranger, he will respond accordingly.

Once the puppy begins to produce hormones, his natural curiosity emerges and he begins to investigate the world around him. It is at this time when you may notice that the untrained dog begins to wander away from you and even ignore your commands to stay close. When this behaviour becomes a problem, the owner has two choices: get rid of the dog or train him. It is strongly urged that you choose the latter option.

There are usually classes within a reasonable distance from the owner's home, but you must also do a lot to train your

TRAINING TIP

Training a dog is a life experience. Many parents admit that much of what they know about raising children they learned from caring for their dogs. Dogs respond to love, fairness and guidance, just as children do. Become a good dog owner and you may become an even better parent.

dog in between classes at home. Sometimes there are classes available but the tuition is too costly. Whatever the circumstances, the solution to your training problems lies within the pages of this book.

This chapter is devoted to helping you train your Bearded Collie at home. If the recommended procedures are followed faithfully, you may expect positive results that will prove rewarding to both you and your dog.

Whether your new charge is a puppy or a mature adult, the methods of teaching and the techniques we use in training basic behaviours are the same. After all, no dog, whether puppy or adult, likes harsh or inhumane methods. All creatures, however, respond favourably to gentle motivational methods and sincere praise and encouragement. Now let us get started.

Consistency is the key to housebreaking your Bearded Collie. Take him to the same place to relieve himself each time and it will become a habit for him.

DID YOU KNOW?
Dogs will do anything for your attention. If you reward the dog when he is calm and resting, you will develop a well-mannered dog. If, on the other hand, you greet your dog excitedly and encourage him to wrestle and roughhouse with you, the dog will greet you the same way and you will have a hyper dog on your hands.

THINK BEFORE YOU BARK
Dogs are sensitive to their master's moods and emotions. Use your voice wisely when communicating with your dog. Never raise your voice at your dog unless you are angry and trying to correct him. 'Barking' at your dog can become as meaningless as 'dogspeak' is to you. Think before you bark!

MEALTIME

Mealtime should be a peaceful time for your puppy. Do not put his food and water bowls in a high-traffic area in the house. For example, give him his own little corner of the kitchen where he can eat undisturbed and where he will not be under foot. Do not allow small children or other family members to disrupt the pup when he is eating.

HOUSEBREAKING

You can train a puppy to relieve itself wherever you choose, but this must be somewhere suitable. You should bear in mind from the outset that when your puppy is old enough to go out in public places, any canine deposits must be removed at once. You will always have to carry with you a small plastic bag or 'poop-scoop.'

Outdoor training includes such surfaces as grass, soil and cement. Indoor training usually means training your dog to newspaper.

When deciding on the surface and location that you will want your Bearded Collie to use, be sure it is going to be permanent. Training your dog to grass and then changing your mind two months later is extremely difficult for both dog and owner.

Next, choose the command you will use each and every time you want your puppy to void.

DID YOU KNOW?

Dogs are the most honourable animals in existence. They consider another species (humans) as their own. They interface with you. You are their leader. Puppies perceive children to be on their level; their actions around small children are different from their behaviour around their adult masters.

'Hurry up' and 'Toilet' are examples of commands commonly used by dog owners.

Get in the habit of giving the puppy your chosen relief command before you take him out. That way, when he becomes an adult, you will be able to determine if he wants to go out when you ask him. A confirmation will be signs of interest, wagging his tail, watching you intently, going to the door, etc.

PUPPY'S NEEDS

Puppy needs to relieve himself after play periods, after each meal, after he has been sleeping and at any time he indicates that he is looking for a place to urinate or defecate.

The urinary and intestinal

> ### HOW MANY TIMES A DAY?
>
> | AGE | RELIEF TRIPS |
> | --- | --- |
> | To 14 weeks | 10 |
> | 14–22 weeks | 8 |
> | 22–32 weeks | 6 |
> | Adulthood | 4 |
> | (dog stops growing) | |
>
> These are estimates, of course, but they are a guide to the MINIMUM opportunities a dog should have each day to relieve itself.

tract muscles of very young puppies are not fully developed. Therefore, like human babies, puppies need to relieve themselves frequently.

Take your puppy out often—every hour for an eight-week-old, for example, and always immediately after sleeping and eating. The older the puppy, the less often he will need to relieve himself. Finally, as a mature healthy adult, he will require only three to five relief trips per day.

HOUSING

Since the types of housing and control you provide for your puppy have a direct relationship on the success of housetraining, we consider the various aspects of both before we begin training.

Bringing a new puppy home and turning him loose in your house can be compared to turning

> ### HOUSEBREAKING TIP
>
> Most of all, be consistent. Always take your dog to the same location, always use the same command, and always have him on lead when he is in his relief area, unless a fenced-in garden is available.
>
> By following the Success Method, your puppy will be completely housetrained by the time his muscle and brain development reach maturity. Keep in mind that small breeds usually mature faster than large breeds, but all puppies should be trained by six months of age.

Canine Development Schedule

It is important to understand how and at what age a puppy develops into adulthood.
If you are a puppy owner, consult the following Canine Development Schedule to
determine the stage of development your puppy is currently experiencing.
This knowledge will help you as you work with the puppy in the weeks and months ahead.

Period	Age	Characteristics
FIRST TO THIRD	**BIRTH TO SEVEN WEEKS**	Puppy needs food, sleep and warmth, and responds to simple and gentle touching. Needs mother for security and disciplining. Needs littermates for learning and interacting with other dogs. Pup learns to function within a pack and learns pack order of dominance. Begin socialising with adults and children for short periods. Begins to become aware of its environment.
FOURTH	**EIGHT TO TWELVE WEEKS**	Brain is fully developed. Needs socialising with outside world. Remove from mother and littermates. Needs to change from canine pack to human pack. Human dominance necessary. Fear period occurs between 8 and 16 weeks. Avoid fright and pain.
FIFTH	**THIRTEEN TO SIXTEEN WEEKS**	Training and formal obedience should begin. Less association with other dogs, more with people, places, situations. Period will pass easily if you remember this is pup's change-to-adolescence time. Be firm and fair. Flight instinct prominent. Permissiveness and over-disciplining can do permanent damage. Praise for good behaviour.
JUVENILE	**FOUR TO EIGHT MONTHS**	Another fear period about 7 to 8 months of age. It passes quickly, but be cautious of fright and pain. Sexual maturity reached. Dominant traits established. Dog should understand sit, down, come and stay by now.

NOTE: THESE ARE APPROXIMATE TIME FRAMES. ALLOW FOR INDIVIDUAL DIFFERENCES IN PUPPIES.

a child loose in a sports arena and telling the child that the place is all his! The sheer enormity of the place would be too much for him to handle.

Instead, offer the puppy clearly defined areas where he can play, sleep, eat and live. A room of the house where the family gathers is the most obvious choice. Puppies are social animals and need to feel a part of the pack right from the start. Hearing your voice, watching you whilst you are doing things and smelling you nearby are all positive reinforcers that he is now a member of your pack. Usually a family room, the kitchen or a nearby adjoining breakfast area is ideal for providing safety and security for both puppy and owner.

Within that room there

TRAINING TIP

Your dog is actually training you at the same time you are training him. Dogs do things to get attention. They usually repeat whatever succeeds in getting your attention.

should be a smaller area which the puppy can call his own. An alcove, a wire or fibreglass dog crate or a fenced (not boarded!) corner from which he can view the activities of his new family will be fine. The size of the area or crate is the key factor here. The area must be large enough for the

DID YOU KNOW?

Never line your pup's sleeping area with newspaper. Puppy litters are usually raised on newspaper and, once in your home, the puppy will immediately associate newspaper with voiding. Never put newspaper on any floor while housetraining, as this will only confuse the puppy. If you are paper-training him, use paper in his designated relief area ONLY. Finally, restrict water intake after evening meals. Offer a few licks at a time—never let a young puppy gulp water after meals.

puppy to lie down and stretch out as well as stand up without rubbing his head on the top, yet small enough so that he cannot relieve himself at one end and sleep at the other without coming into contact with his droppings until fully trained to relieve himself outside.

Dogs are, by nature, clean animals and will not remain close to their relief areas unless forced to do so. In those cases, they then become dirty dogs and usually remain that way for life.

The designated area should be lined with clean bedding and a toy. Water must always be available, in a non-spill container.

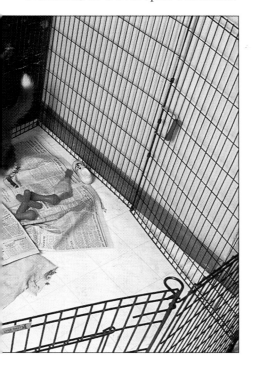

CONTROL

By control, we mean helping the puppy to create a lifestyle pattern that will be compatible to that of his human pack (YOU!). Just as we guide little children to learn our way of life, we must show the puppy when it is time to play, eat, sleep, exercise and even entertain himself.

Your puppy should always sleep in his crate. He should also learn that, during times of household confusion and excessive human activity such as at breakfast when family members are preparing for the day, he can play by himself in relative safety and comfort in his designated area. Each time you leave the puppy alone, he should understand exactly where he is to stay. Puppies are chewers. They cannot tell the difference between lamp cords, television wires, shoes, table legs, etc. Chewing into a television wire, for example, can be fatal to the puppy

Most breeders begin the housebreaking process before the litter leaves their home or kennel. Newspaper lining is usually associated with toilet habits, so never use it in your pup's crate or sleeping area.

TRAINING TIP

Stand up straight and authoritatively when giving your dog commands. Do not issue commands when lying on the floor or lying on your back on the sofa. If you are on your hands and knees when you give a command, your dog will think you are positioning yourself to play.

whilst a shorted wire can start a fire in the house.

If the puppy chews on the arm of the chair when he is alone, you will probably discipline him angrily when you get home. Thus, he makes the association that your coming home means he is going to be punished. (He will not remember chewing up the chair and is incapable of making the association of the discipline with his naughty deed.)

Other times of excitement, such as family parties, etc., can be fun for the puppy providing he can view the activities from the security of his designated area. He is not underfoot and he is not being fed all sorts of titbits that will probably cause him stomach distress, yet he still feels a part of the fun.

SCHEDULE

A puppy should be taken to his relief area each time he is released

HOUSEBREAKING TIP
Do not carry your dog to his toilet area. Lead him there on a leash or, better yet, encourage him to follow you to the spot. If you start carrying him to his spot, you might end up doing this routine forever and your dog will have the satisfaction of having trained YOU.

from his designated area, after meals, after a play session, when he first awakens in the morning (at age eight weeks, this can mean 5 a.m.!). The puppy will indicate that he's ready 'to go' by circling or sniffing busily—do not misinterpret these signs. For a puppy less than ten weeks of age, a routine of taking him out every hour is necessary. As the puppy grows, he will be able to wait for longer periods of time.

Keep trips to his relief area short. Stay no more than five or six minutes and then return to the house. If he goes during that time, praise him lavishly and take him indoors immediately. If he does not, but he has an accident when you go back indoors, pick him up immediately, say 'No! No!' and return to his relief area. Wait a few minutes, then return to the house again. Never hit a puppy or rub his face in urine or excrement when he has an accident! Once indoors, put the puppy

THE GOLDEN RULE
The golden rule of dog training is simple. For each 'question' (command), there is only one correct answer (reaction). One command = one reaction. Keep practising the command until the dog reacts correctly without hesitating. Be repetitive but not monotonous.
Dogs get bored just as people do!

THE SUCCESS METHOD

Success that comes by luck is usually short lived. Success that comes by well-thought-out proven methods is often more easily achieved and permanent. This is the Success Method. It is designed to give you, the puppy owner, a simple yet proven way to help your puppy develop clean living habits and a feeling of security in his new environment.

in his crate until you have had time to clean up his accident. Then release him to the family area and watch him more closely than before. Chances are, his accident was a result of your not picking up his signal or waiting too long before offering him the opportunity to relieve himself. Never hold a grudge against the puppy for accidents.

Let the puppy learn that going outdoors means it is time to relieve himself, not play. Once trained, he will be able to play indoors and out and still differentiate between the times for play versus the times for relief.

Help him develop regular hours for naps, being alone, playing by himself and just resting, all in his crate. Encourage him to entertain himself whilst you are busy with your activities. Let him learn that having you

PRACTICE MAKES PERFECT!

• Have training lessons with your dog every day in several short segments—three to five times a day for a few minutes at a time is ideal.
• Do not have long practice sessions. The dog will become easily bored.
• Never practise when you are tired, ill, worried or in an otherwise negative mood. This will transmit to the dog and may have an adverse effect on its performance.

Think fun, short and above all POSITIVE! End each session on a high note, rather than a failed exercise, and make sure to give a lot of praise. Enjoy the training and help your dog enjoy it, too.

Puppies will often sniff around before they relieve themselves. Upon locating a 'familiar' scent (where the pup or another dog relieved himself), the pup will do accordingly.

95

near is comforting, but it is not your main purpose in life to provide him with undivided attention.

Each time you put a puppy in his own area, use the same command, whatever suits best. Soon, he will run to his crate or special area when he hears you say those words.

Crate training provides safety for you, the puppy and the home. It also provides the puppy with a feeling of security, and that helps the puppy achieve self-confidence and clean habits.

Remember that one of the

DID YOU KNOW?

By providing sleeping and resting quarters that fit the dog, and offering frequent opportunities to relieve himself outside his quarters, the puppy quickly learns that the outdoors (or the newspaper if you are training him to paper) is the place to go when he needs to urinate or defecate. It also reinforces his innate desire to keep his sleeping quarters clean. This, in turn, helps develop the muscle control that will eventually produce a dog with clean living habits.

THE SUCCESS METHOD
6 Steps to Successful Crate Training

1 Tell the puppy 'Crate time!' and place him in the crate with a small treat (a piece of cheese or half of a biscuit). Let him stay in the crate for five minutes while you are in the same room. Then release him and praise lavishly. Never release him when he is fussing. Wait until he is quiet before you let him out.

2 Repeat Step 1 several times a day.

3 The next day, place the puppy in the crate as before. Let him stay there for ten minutes. Do this several times.

4 Continue building time in five-minute increments until the puppy

stays in his crate for 30 minutes with you in the room. Always take him to his relief area after prolonged periods in his crate.

5 Now go back to Step 1 and let the puppy stay in his crate for five minutes, this time while you are out of the room.

6 Once again, build crate time in five-minute increments with you out of the room. When the puppy will stay willingly in his crate (he may even fall asleep!) for 30 minutes with you out of the room, he will be ready to stay in it for several hours at a time.

Cleanliness is next to godliness— always pick up after your dog.

training is the answer for now and in the future.

In conclusion, a few key elements are really all you need for a successful house training method—consistency, frequency, praise, control and supervision. By following these procedures with a normal, healthy puppy, you and the puppy will soon be past the stage of 'accidents' and ready to move on to a full and rewarding life together.

Never carry your puppy outdoors to relieve himself during house-breaking. Let the pup make his way to his designated area on his own. You can guide him by using the chosen relief command.

ROLES OF DISCIPLINE, REWARD AND PUNISHMENT

Discipline, training one to act in accordance with rules, brings

primary ingredients in housetraining your puppy is control. Regardless of your lifestyle, there will always be occasions when you will need to have a place where your dog can stay and be happy and safe. Crate

97

If you train your Bearded Collie correctly, he will become a well-mannered dog that is a pleasure to take with you wherever you go.

TRAINING TIP

Never train your dog, puppy or adult, when you are mad or in a sour mood. Dogs are very sensitive to human feelings, especially anger, and if your dog senses that you are angry or upset, he will connect your anger with his training and learn to resent or fear his training sessions.

DID YOU KNOW?

Dogs do not understand our language. They can be trained to react to a certain sound, at a certain volume. If you say 'No, Oliver' in a very soft pleasant voice it will not have the same meaning as 'No, Oliver!!' when you shout it as loud as you can. You should never use the dog's name during a reprimand, just the command NO!! Since dogs don't understand words, comics often use dogs trained with opposite meanings. Thus, when the comic commands his dog to SIT the dog will stand up, and vice versa.

order to life. It is as simple as that. Without discipline, particularly in a group society, chaos reigns supreme and the group will eventually perish. Humans and canines are social animals and need some form of discipline in order to function effectively. They must procure food, protect their home base and their young and reproduce to keep the species going.

If there were no discipline in the lives of social animals, they would eventually die from starvation and/or predation by other stronger animals.

In the case of domestic canines, dogs need discipline in their lives in order to understand how their pack (you and other family members) functions and how they must act in order to survive.

A large humane society in a highly populated area recently surveyed dog owners regarding their satisfaction with their relationships with their dogs. People who had trained their dogs were 75% more satisfied with their pets than those who had never trained their dogs.

Dr Edward Thorndike, a psychologist, established *Thorndike's Theory of Learning*, which states that a behaviour that results in a pleasant event tends to be repeated. A behaviour that results in an unpleasant event tends not to be repeated. It is this theory on which training methods are based today. For example, if you manipulate a dog to perform a specific behaviour and reward him for doing it, he is likely to do it again because he enjoyed the end result.

Occasionally, punishment, a penalty inflicted for an offence, is necessary. The best type of punishment often comes from an outside source. For example, a child is told not to touch the stove because he may get burned. He disobeys and touches the stove. In doing so, he receives a burn. From that time on, he respects the heat of the stove and avoids contact with it. Therefore, a behaviour that results in an unpleasant event tends not to be repeated.

A good example of a dog learning the hard way is the dog who chases the house cat. He is told many times to leave the cat alone, yet he persists in teasing the cat. Then, one day he begins chasing the cat but the cat turns

and swipes a claw across the dog's face, leaving him with a painful gash on his nose. The final result is that the dog stops chasing the cat.

TRAINING EQUIPMENT
COLLAR AND LEAD
For a Bearded Collie the collar and lead that you use for training must be one with which you are easily able to work, not too heavy for the dog and perfectly safe.

Your Beardie puppy's training collar should be safe, comfortable, and easy to work with. Accustom the pup to the collar before you are ready to initiate the first lesson.

DID YOU KNOW?
Dogs are as different from each other as people are. What works for one dog may not work for another. Have an open mind. If one method of training is unsuccessful, try another.

TREATS

Have a bag of treats on hand. Something nutritious and easy to swallow works best. Use a soft treat, a chunk of cheese or a piece of cooked chicken rather than a dry biscuit. By the time the dog has finished chewing a dry treat, he will forget why he is being rewarded in the first place! Using food rewards will not teach a dog to beg at the table—the only way to teach a dog to beg at the table is to give him food from the table. In

learn anything if he is looking away from you with his mind on something else.

To get his attention, ask him, 'School?' and immediately walk over to him and give him a treat as you tell him 'Good dog.' Wait a minute or two and repeat the routine, this time with a treat in your hand as you approach within a foot of the dog. Do not go directly to him, but stop about a foot short of him and hold out the treat as you ask, 'School?' He will

When training with treats, use something soft and easy to chew. By the time the puppy is finished chewing a dried treat, he may forget why he is being rewarded.

training, rewarding the dog with a food treat will help him associate praise and the treats with learning new behaviours that obviously please his owner.

TRAINING BEGINS: ASK THE DOG A QUESTION

In order to teach your dog anything, you must first get his attention. After all, he cannot

see you approaching with a treat in your hand and most likely begin walking toward you. As you meet, give him the treat and praise again.

The third time, ask the question, have a treat in your hand and walk only a short distance toward the dog so that he must walk almost all the way to you. As he reaches you, give him the treat and praise again.

By this time, the dog will probably be getting the idea that if he pays attention to you, especially when you ask that question, it will pay off in treats and enjoyable activities for him. In other words, he learns that 'school' means doing enjoyable things with you that result in treats and positive attention for him.

Remember that the dog does not understand your verbal language, he only recognises sounds. Your question translates to a series of sounds for him, and those sounds become the signal to go to you and pay attention; if he does, he will get to interact with you plus receive treats and praise.

THE BASIC COMMANDS
TEACHING SIT

Now that you have the dog's attention, attach his lead and hold it in your left hand and a food treat in your right. Place your food hand at the dog's nose and let him lick the treat but not take it from you. Say 'Sit' and slowly raise your food hand from in front of the dog's nose up over his head so that he is looking at the ceiling. As he bends his head upward, he will have to bend his knees to maintain his balance. As he bends his knees, he will assume a sit position. At that point, release the food treat and praise lavishly with comments such as 'Good dog!

Good sit!', etc. Remember to always praise enthusiastically, because dogs relish verbal praise from their owners and feel so proud of themselves whenever they accomplish a behaviour.

You will not use food forever in getting the dog to obey your commands. Food is only used to teach new behaviours, and once the dog knows what you want

As you say 'Sit,' raise your hand with the treat in it; as he looks upward toward the treat he will bend his knees and...*voila*...the sit position is assumed.

If a treat is not working, you may have to push down on your Bearded Collie's rear in order to get him to sit. This method is the less desirable approach, but it does work for some stubborn Beardies.

when you give a specific command, you will wean him off the food treats but still maintain the verbal praise. After all, you will always have your voice with you, and there will be many times when you have no food rewards but expect the dog to obey.

DID YOU KNOW?

A dog in jeopardy never lies down. He stays alert on his feet because instinct tells him that he may have to run away or fight for his survival. Therefore, if a dog feels threatened or anxious, he will not lie down. Consequently, it is important to have the dog calm and relaxed as he learns the down exercise.

TEACHING DOWN

Teaching the down exercise is easy when you understand how the dog perceives the down position, and it is very difficult when you do not. Dogs perceive the down position as a submissive one, therefore teaching the down exercise using a forceful method can sometimes make the dog develop such a fear of the down that he either runs away when you say 'Down' or he attempts to snap at the person who tries to force him down.

Have the dog sit close alongside your left leg, facing in the same direction as you are. Hold the lead in your left hand and a food treat in your right. Now place your left hand lightly on the top of the dog's shoulders where they meet above the spinal cord. Do not push down on the dog's shoulders; simply rest your left hand there so you can guide the dog to lie down close to your left leg rather than to swing away from your side when he drops.

Now place the food hand at the dog's nose, say 'Down' very softly (almost a whisper), and slowly lower the food hand to the dog's front feet. When the food hand reaches the floor, begin moving it forward along the floor in front of the dog. Keep talking softly to the dog, saying things like, 'Do you want this treat? You can do this, good dog.' Your reassuring tone of voice will help calm the dog as he tries to follow the food hand in order to get the treat.

When the dog's elbows touch the floor, release the food and praise softly. Try to get the dog to maintain that down position for several seconds before you let him sit up again. The goal here is to get the dog to settle down and not feel threatened in the down position.

TEACHING STAY

It is easy to teach the dog to stay in either a sit or a down position.

Again, we use food and praise during the teaching process as we help the dog to understand exactly what it is that we are expecting him to do.

To teach the sit/stay, start with the dog sitting on your left side as before and hold the lead in your left hand. Have a food treat in your right hand and place your food hand at the dog's nose. Say 'Stay' and step out on your right foot to stand directly in front of the dog, toe to toe, as he licks and nibbles the treat. Be sure to keep his head facing upward to

Whenever your Bearded Collie successfully completes a command, offer him a treat and lots of praise. This dog is in the down position. Keeping the dog's attention is half the battle!

Bearded Collie

maintain the sit position. Count to five and then swing around to stand next to the dog again with him on your left. As soon as you get back to the original position, release the food and praise lavishly.

To teach the down/stay, do the down as previously described. As soon as the dog lies down, say

'Stay' and step out on your right foot just as you did in the sit/stay. Count to five and then return to stand beside the dog with him on your left side. Release the treat and praise as always.

Within a week or ten days, you can begin to add a bit of distance between you and your dog when you leave him. When you do, use your left hand open with the palm facing the dog as a stay signal, much the same as the hand signal a police officer uses to stop traffic at an intersection. Hold the food treat in your right hand as before, but this time the food is not touching the dog's nose. He will watch the food hand and quickly learn that he is going to get that treat as soon as you return to his side.

When you can stand 1 metre away from your dog for 30 seconds, you can then begin building time and distance in both stays. Eventually, the dog

can be expected to remain in the stay position for prolonged periods of time until you return to him or call him to you. Always praise lavishly when he stays.

TEACHING COME

If you make teaching 'come' a fun experience, you should never have a 'student' that does not love the game or that fails to come when called. The secret, it seems, is never to teach the word 'come.'

At times when an owner most wants his dog to come when called, the owner is likely to be upset or anxious and he allows these feelings to come through in the tone of his voice when he calls his dog. Hearing that desperation in his owner's voice, the dog fears the results of going to him and therefore either disobeys outright or runs in the opposite direction. The secret, therefore, is to teach the dog a game and, when you want him to come to you, simply play the game. It is practically a no-fail solution!

To begin, have several

It is important to make teaching 'Come' an enjoyable experience for your dog, as this is the most important command and could save your Bearded Collie's life one day.

members of your family take a few food treats and each go into a different room in the house. Take turns calling the dog, and each person should celebrate the dog's finding him with a treat and lots of happy praise. When a person calls the dog, he is actually inviting the dog to find him and get a treat as a reward for 'winning.'

A few turns of the 'Where are you?' game and the dog will understand that everyone is playing the game and that each person has a big celebration awaiting his success at locating them. Once he learns to love the game, simply calling out 'Where are you?' will bring him running from wherever he is when he hears that all-important question.

The come command is recognised as one of the most important things to teach a dog, but there are trainers who work with thousands of dogs and never teach the actual word 'Come.' Yet

TRAINING TIP
Teach your dog to HEEL in an enclosed area. Once you think the dog will obey reliably and you want to attempt advanced obedience exercises such as off-lead heeling, test him in a fenced-in area so he cannot run away.

these dogs will race to respond to a person who uses the dog's name followed by 'Where are you?' For example, a woman has a 12-year-old companion dog who went blind, but who never fails to locate her owner when asked, 'Where are you?'

Children particularly love to play this game with their dogs. Children can hide in smaller places like a shower or bath, behind a bed or under a table. The dog needs to work a little bit harder to find these hiding places, but when he does he loves to celebrate with a treat and a tussle with a favourite youngster.

TEACHING HEEL
Heeling means that the dog walks beside the owner without pulling. It takes time and patience on the owner's part to succeed at teaching the dog that he (the owner) will not proceed unless the dog is walking calmly beside him. Pulling out ahead on the lead is definitely not acceptable.

DID YOU KNOW?
Play fetch games with your puppy in an enclosed area where he can retrieve his toy and bring it back to you. Always use a toy or object designated just for this purpose. Never use a shoe, stocking or other item he may later confuse with those in your wardrobe or underneath your chair.

Begin with holding the lead in your left hand as the dog sits beside your left leg. Move the loop end of the lead to your right hand but keep your left hand short on the lead so it keeps the dog in close next to you.

Say 'Heel' and step forward on your left foot. Keep the dog close to you and take three steps. Stop and have the dog sit next to you in what we now call the 'heel position.' Praise verbally, but do not touch the dog. Hesitate a moment and begin again with 'Heel,' taking three steps and stopping, at which point the dog is told to sit again.

Your goal here is to have the dog walk those three steps without pulling on the lead. When he will walk calmly beside you for three steps without pulling, increase the number of steps you take to five. When he will walk politely beside you whilst you take five steps, you can increase the length of your walk to ten steps. Keep increasing the length of your stroll until the dog will walk quietly beside you without pulling as long as you want him to heel. When you stop heeling, indicate to the dog that the exercise is over by verbally praising as you pet him and say 'OK, good dog.' The 'OK' is used as a release word meaning that the exercise is finished and the dog is free to relax.

If you are dealing with a dog

TRAINING TIP

If you begin teaching the heel by taking long walks and letting the dog pull you along, he misinterprets this action as an acceptable form of taking a walk. When you pull back on the lead to counteract his pulling, he reads that tug as a signal to pull even harder!

Heeling is when the dog walks beside the owner without pulling. Once a Bearded Collie learns to heel properly, even a child could handle walking him.

TRAINING TIP
If you are walking your dog and he suddenly stops and looks straight into your eyes, ignore him. Pull the leash and lead him into the direction you want to walk.

who insists on pulling you around, simply 'put on your brakes' and stand your ground until the dog realises that the two of you are not going anywhere until he is beside you and moving at your pace, not his. It may take some time just standing there to convince the dog that you are the leader and you will be the one to decide on the direction and speed of your travel.

Each time the dog looks up at you or slows down to give a slack lead between the two of you, quietly praise him and say, 'Good heel. Good dog.' Eventually, the dog will begin to respond and within a few days he will be walking politely beside you without pulling on the lead. At first, the training sessions should be kept short and very positive; soon the dog will be able to walk nicely with you for increasingly longer distances. Remember also to give the dog free time and the opportunity to run and play when you have finished heel practice.

WEANING OFF FOOD IN TRAINING

Food is used in training new behaviours. Once the dog understands what behaviour goes with a specific command, it is time to start weaning him off the food treats. At first, give a treat after each exercise. Then, start to give a treat only after every other exercise. Mix up the times when

DID YOU KNOW?
If you have other pets in the home and/or interact often with the pets of friends and other family members, your pup will respond to those pets in much the same manner as you do. It is only when you show fear of or resentment toward another animal that he will act fearful or unfriendly.

OBEDIENCE SCHOOL

A basic obedience beginner's class usually lasts for six to eight weeks. Dog and owner attend an hour-long lesson once a week and practise for a few minutes, several times a day, each day at home. If done properly, the whole procedure will result in a well-mannered dog and an owner who delights in living with a pet that is eager to please and enjoys doing things with his owner.

Agility is a terrific sport where dogs run through an obstacle course. Bearded Collies have a natural aptitude for agility due to their superior balance and their desire to please. This Beardie is crossing over the see-saw.

you offer a food reward and the times when you only offer praise so that the dog will never know when he is going to receive both food and praise and when he is going to receive only praise. This is called a variable ratio reward system and it proves successful because there is always the chance that the owner will produce a treat,

DID YOU KNOW?
Occasionally, a dog and owner who have not attended formal classes have been able to earn entry-level titles by obtaining competition rules and regulations from a local kennel club and practising on their own to a degree of perfection. Obtaining the higher level titles, however, almost always requires extensive training under the tutelage of experienced instructors. In addition, the more difficult levels require more specialised equipment whereas the lower levels do not.

This Bearded Collie sails over the bar jump at an agility trial.

so the dog never stops trying for that reward. No matter what, ALWAYS give verbal praise.

OBEDIENCE CLASSES

It is a good idea to enrol in an obedience class if one is available in your area. If yours is a show dog, ringcraft classes would be more appropriate. Many areas have dog clubs that offer basic obedience training as well as preparatory classes for obedience competition. There are also local dog trainers who offer similar classes.

At obedience trials, dogs can earn titles at various levels of competition. The beginning levels of competition include basic behaviours such as sit, down, heel, etc. The more advanced levels of competition include jumping, retrieving, scent discrimination and signal work. The advanced levels require a dog and owner to put a lot of time and effort into their training and the titles that can

OBEDIENCE SCHOOL

Taking your dog to an obedience school may be the best investment in time and money you can ever make. You will enjoy the benefits for the lifetime of your dog and you will have the opportunity to meet people with your similar expectations for companion dogs.

be earned at these levels of competition are very prestigious.

OTHER ACTIVITIES FOR LIFE

Whether a dog is trained in the structured environment of a class or alone with his owner at home, there are many activities that can bring fun and rewards to both owner and dog once they have mastered basic control.

Teaching the dog to help out around the home, in the garden or on the farm provides great satisfaction to both dog and owner. In addition, the dog's help makes life a little easier for his owner and raises his stature as a valued companion to his family. It helps give the dog a purpose by occupying his mind and providing an outlet for his energy.

Backpacking is an exciting and healthy activity that the dog can be taught without assistance from more than his owner. The exercise of walking and climbing is good for man and dog alike, and the bond that they develop together is priceless.

If you are interested in participating in organised competition with your Bearded Collie, there are activities other than obedience in which you and your dog can become involved. Agility is a popular and exciting sport where dogs run through an obstacle course that includes various jumps, tunnels and other exercises to test the dog's speed and coordination. Beardies, with their exuberance and energy, seem to have a natural aptitude for agility work. The owners run through the course beside their dogs to give commands and to guide them through the course. Although competitive, the focus is on fun—it's fun to do, fun to watch, and great exercise.

At agility trials owners run through the course and give their dogs commands to guide them successfully through the course. One of the most challenging for the enthusiastic Beardie is the 30-second pause.

Dogs suffer many of the same physical illnesses as people. They might even share many of the same psychological problems. Since people usually know more about human diseases than canine maladies, many of the terms used in this chapter will be familiar but not necessarily those used by veterinary surgeons. We will use the term *x-ray*, instead of the more acceptable term *radiograph*. We will also use the familiar term *symptoms* even though dogs don't have symptoms, which are verbal descriptions of the patient's feelings: dogs have *clinical signs*. Since dogs can't speak, we have to look for clinical signs...but we still use the term symptoms in this book.

As a general rule, medicine is practised. That term is not arbitrary. Medicine is a constantly changing art as we learn more and more about

Your chosen veterinary surgeon should be familiar with the latest technologies and have all the necessary equipment at his disposal.

genetics, electronic aids (like CAT scans) and daily laboratory advances. There are many dog maladies, like canine hip dysplasia, which are not universally treated in the same manner. Some veterinary surgeons opt for surgery more often than others do.

SELECTING A VETERINARY SURGEON

Your selection of a veterinary surgeon should not be based upon personality (as most are) but upon their convenience to your home. You want a vet who is close because you might have emergencies or need to make multiple visits for treatments. You want a vet who has services that you might require such as tattooing and grooming facilities, as well as sophisticated pet supplies and a good reputation for ability and responsiveness. There is nothing more frustrating than having to wait a day or more to get a response from your veterinary surgeon.

All veterinary surgeons are licensed and their diplomas and/or certificates should be displayed in their waiting rooms. There are, however, many veterinary specialities that usually require further studies and internships. There are specialists in heart problems (veterinary cardiologists), skin problems (veterinary dermatologists), teeth and gum problems (veterinary dentists), eye problems (veterinary ophthalmologists), X-rays (veterinary radiologists), and surgeons who have specialities in bones, muscles or other organs. Most veterinary surgeons do routine surgery such as neutering, stitching up wounds and docking tails for those breeds in which such is required for show purposes. When the problem affecting your dog is serious, it is not unusual or impudent to get another medical opinion,

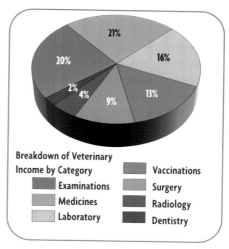

Breakdown of Veterinary Income by Category

- Examinations
- Medicines
- Laboratory
- Vaccinations
- Surgery
- Radiology
- Dentistry

A typical American vet's income categorised according to services provided. This survey dealt with small-animal practices.

although in Britain you are obliged to advise the vets concerned about this. You might also want to compare costs amongst several veterinary surgeons. Sophisticated health care and veterinary services can be very costly. Don't be bashful about discussing these costs with your veterinary surgeon or his (her) staff. It is not infrequent that important decisions are based upon financial considerations.

PREVENTATIVE MEDICINE

It is much easier, less costly and more effective to practise preventative medicine than to fight bouts of illness and disease. Properly bred puppies come from parents that were selected based upon their genetic disease profile. Their mothers should have been vaccinated, free of all internal and external parasites, and properly

DID YOU KNOW?

Male dogs are neutered. The operation removes the testicles and requires that the dog be anaesthetised. Recovery takes about one week. Females are spayed. This is major surgery and it usually takes a bitch two weeks to recover.

nourished. For these reasons, a visit to the veterinary surgeon who cared for the dam (mother) is recommended. The dam can pass on disease resistance to her puppies, which can last for eight to ten weeks. She can also pass on parasites and many infections. That's why you should visit the veterinary surgeon who cared for the dam.

WEANING TO FIVE MONTHS OLD
Puppies should be weaned by the time they are about two months old. A puppy that remains for at least eight weeks with its mother and litter mates usually adapts better to other dogs and people later in its life.

Some new owners have their puppy examined by a veterinary surgeon immediately, which is a good idea. Vaccination programmes usually begin when the puppy is very young.

The puppy will have its teeth examined and have its skeletal conformation and general health checked prior to certification by

> **DID YOU KNOW?**
> The myth that dogs need extra fat in their diets can be harmful. Should your vet recommend extra fat, use safflower oil instead of animal oils. Safflower oil has been shown to be less likely to cause allergic reactions.

> **DID YOU KNOW?**
> Cases of hyperactive adrenal glands (Cushing's disease) have been traced to the drinking of highly chlorinated water. Aerate or age your dog's drinking water before offering it.

the veterinary surgeon. Puppies in certain breeds have problems with their kneecaps, eye cataracts and other eye problems, heart murmurs and undescended testicles. They may also have personality problems and your veterinary surgeon might have training in temperament evaluation.

VACCINATION SCHEDULING
Most vaccinations are given by injection and should only be done by a veterinary surgeon. Both he and you should keep a record of the date of the injection, the identification of the vaccine and the amount given. Some vets give a first vaccination at eight weeks, but most dog breeders prefer the course not to commence until about ten weeks because of negating any antibodies passed on by the dam. The vaccination scheduling is usually based on a 15-day cycle. You must take your vet's advice as to when to vaccinate as this may differ according to the vaccine used.

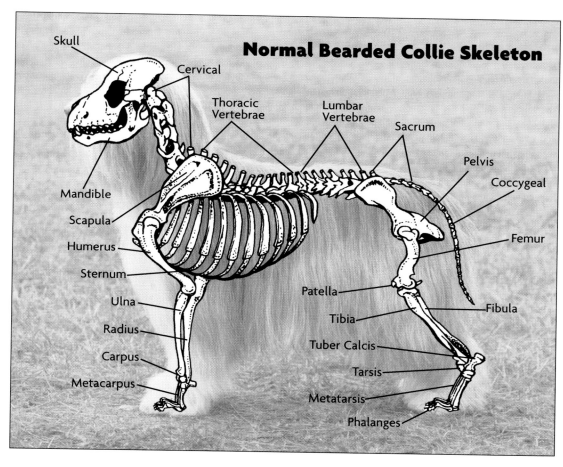

Normal Bearded Collie Skeleton

Skull
Cervical
Thoracic Vertebrae
Lumbar Vertebrae
Sacrum
Pelvis
Coccygeal
Mandible
Scapula
Humerus
Sternum
Femur
Ulna
Patella
Radius
Fibula
Carpus
Tibia
Metacarpus
Tuber Calcis
Tarsis
Metatarsis
Phalanges

Most vaccinations immunise your puppy against viruses.

The usual vaccines contain immunising doses of several different viruses such as distemper, parvovirus, parainfluenza and hepatitis. There are other vaccines available when the puppy is at risk. You should rely upon professional advice. This is especially true for the booster-shot programme. Most vaccination programmes require a booster when the puppy is a

DID YOU KNOW?
Not every dog's ears are the same. Ears that are open to the air are healthier than ears with poor air circulation. Sometimes a dog can have two differently shaped ears. You should not probe inside your dog's ears. Only clean that which is accessible with a soft cotton wipe.

HEALTH AND VACCINATION SCHEDULE

AGE IN WEEKS:	3RD	6TH	8TH	10TH	12TH	14TH	16TH	20-24TH
Worm Control	✔	✔	✔	✔	✔	✔	✔	✔
Neutering								✔
Heartworm*		✔						✔
Parvovirus		✔		✔		✔		✔
Distemper			✔		✔		✔	
Hepatitis			✔		✔		✔	
Leptospirosis		✔		✔		✔		
Parainfluenza		✔		✔		✔		
Dental Examination			✔					✔
Complete Physical			✔					✔
Temperament Testing			✔					
Coronavirus					✔			
Kennel Cough		✔						
Hip Dysplasia							✔	
Rabies*								✔

Vaccinations are not instantly effective. It takes about two weeks for the dog's immunisation system to develop antibodies. Most vaccinations require annual booster shots. Your veterinary surgeon should guide you in this regard.
*Not applicable in the United Kingdom

year old and once a year thereafter. In some cases, circumstances may require more frequent immunisations. Kennel cough, more formally known as tracheobronchitis, is treated with a vaccine that is sprayed into the dog's nostrils. Kennel cough is usually included in routine vaccination, but this is often not so effective as for other major diseases.

FIVE MONTHS TO ONE YEAR OF AGE
Unless you intend to breed or show your dog, neutering the puppy at six months of age is recommended. Discuss this with your veterinary surgeon; most professionals advise neutering

DID YOU KNOW?

Vaccines do not work all the time. Sometimes dogs are allergic to them and many times the antibodies, which are supposed to be stimulated by the vaccine, just are not produced. You should keep your dog in the veterinary clinic for an hour after it is vaccinated to be sure there are no allergic reactions.

the puppy. Neutering has proven to be extremely beneficial to both male and female puppies. Besides eliminating the possibility of pregnancy, it inhibits (but does not prevent) breast cancer in bitches and prostate cancer in male dogs. Under no circumstances should a bitch be spayed prior to her first season.

DOGS OLDER THAN ONE YEAR
Continue to visit the veterinary surgeon at least once a year. There is no such disease as old age, but bodily functions do change with age. The eyes and ears are no longer as efficient. Liver, kidney and intestinal functions often decline. Proper dietary changes, recommended by your veterinary surgeon, can make life more pleasant for the ageing Bearded Collie and you.

Disease	What is it?	What causes it?	Symptoms
Leptospirosis	Severe disease that affects the internal organs; can be spread to people.	A bacterium, which is often carried by rodents, that enters through mucous membranes and spreads quickly throughout the body.	Range from fever, vomiting and loss of appetite in less severe cases to shock, irreversible kidney damage and possibly death in most severe cases.
Rabies	Potentially deadly virus that infects warm-blooded mammals. Not seen in United Kingdom.	Bite from a carrier of the virus, mainly wild animals.	1st stage: dog exhibits change in behaviour, fear. 2nd stage: dog's behaviour becomes more aggressive. 3rd stage: loss of coordination, trouble with bodily functions.
Parvovirus	Highly contagious virus, potentially deadly.	Ingestion of the virus, which is usually spread through the faeces of infected dogs.	Most common: severe diarrhoea. Also vomiting, fatigue, lack of appetite.
Kennel cough	Contagious respiratory infection.	Combination of types of bacteria and virus. Most common: *Bordetella bronchiseptica* bacteria and parainfluenza virus.	Chronic cough.
Distemper	Disease primarily affecting respiratory and nervous system.	Virus that is related to the human measles virus.	Mild symptoms such as fever, lack of appetite and mucous secretion progress to evidence of brain damage, 'hard pad.'
Hepatitis	Virus primarily affecting the liver.	Canine adenovirus type I (CAV-1). Enters system when dog breathes in particles.	Lesser symptoms include listlessness, diarrhoea, vomiting. More severe symptoms include 'blue-eye' (clumps of virus in eye).
Coronavirus	Virus resulting in digestive problems.	Virus is spread through infected dog's faeces.	Stomach upset evidenced by lack of appetite, vomiting, diarrhoea.

ACRODERMATITIS

There is a 25% chance of a puppy getting this fatal gene combination from two parents with recessive genes for acrodermatitis:

AA= NORMAL, HEALTHY
aa= FATAL
Aa= RECESSIVE, NORMAL APPEARING

If the female parent has an Aa gene and the male parent has an Aa gene, the chances are one in four that the puppy will have the fatal genetic combination aa.

Sire \ Dam	A	a	♀
A	AA	Aa	
a	Aa	aa	
♂			

SKIN PROBLEMS IN BEARDED COLLIES

Veterinary surgeons are consulted by dog owners for skin problems more than any other group of diseases or maladies. Dogs' skin is almost as sensitive as human skin and both suffer almost the same ailments (though the occurrence of acne in dogs is rare!). For this reason, veterinary dermatology has developed into a speciality practised by many veterinary surgeons.

Since many skin problems have visual symptoms that are almost identical, it requires the skill of an experienced veterinary dermatologist to identify and cure many of the more severe skin disorders. Pet shops sell many treatments for skin problems but most of the treatments are directed at symptoms and not the underlying problem(s). If your dog is suffering from a skin disorder, you should seek professional assistance as quickly as possible. As with all diseases, the earlier a problem is identified and treated, the more successful is the cure.

INHERITED SKIN PROBLEMS

Many skin disorders are inherited and some are fatal. For example,

acrodermatitis is an inherited disease that is transmitted by both parents. The parents, who appear (phenotypically) normal, have a recessive gene for acrodermatitis, meaning that they carry, but are not affected by the disease.

Acrodermatitis is just one example of how difficult it is to prevent congenital dog diseases. The cost and skills required to ascertain whether two dogs should be mated are too high even though puppies with acrodermatitis rarely reach two years of age.

Other inherited skin problems are usually not as fatal as acrodermatitis. All inherited diseases must be diagnosed and treated by

a veterinary specialist. There are active programmes being undertaken by many veterinary pharmaceutical manufacturers to solve most, if not all, of the common skin problems of dogs.

PARASITE BITES
Many of us are allergic to insect bites. The bites itch, erupt and may even become infected. Dogs have the same reaction to fleas, ticks and/or mites. When an insect lands on you, you have the chance to whisk it away with your hand. Unfortunately, when our dog is bitten by a flea, tick or mite, it can

DID YOU KNOW?
A dental examination is in order when the dog is between six months and one year of age so any permanent teeth that have erupted incorrectly can be corrected. It is important to begin a brushing routine, preferably using a two-sided brushing technique, whereby both sides of the tooth are brushed at the same time. Durable nylon and safe edible chews should be a part of your puppy's arsenal for good health, good teeth and pleasant breath. The vast majority of dogs three to four years old and older has diseases of the gums from lack of dental attention. Using the various types of dental chews can be very effective in controlling dental plaque.

As much as your Bearded Collie loves to be outside, you must make sure that he is properly protected from fleas, ticks, and other parasites that can jump on him outdoors.

only scratch it away or bite it. By the time the dog has been bitten, the parasite has done some of its damage. It may also have laid eggs to cause further problems in the near future. The itching from parasite bites is probably due to the saliva injected into the site when the parasite sucks the dog's blood.

AUTO-IMMUNE SKIN CONDITIONS
Auto-immune skin conditions are commonly referred to as being allergic to yourself, whilst allergies are usually inflammatory reactions to an outside stimulus. Auto-immune diseases cause serious damage to the tissues that are involved.

The best known auto-immune disease is lupus, which affects people as well as dogs. The symptoms are variable and may affect the kidneys, bones, blood chemistry and skin. It can be fatal to both dogs and humans, though it is not thought to be transmissible. It is usually successfully treated with cortisone, prednisone or similar corticosteroid, but extensive use of these drugs can have harmful side effects.

AIRBORNE ALLERGIES
An interesting allergy, which often causes skin problems and irritations in dogs, is pollen allergy. Humans have hay fever, rose fever and other fevers with

which they suffer during the pollinating season. Many dogs suffer the same allergies. When the pollen count is high, your dog might suffer but don't expect them to sneeze and have runny noses like humans. Dogs react to pollen allergies the same way they react to fleas—they scratch and bite themselves.

Dogs, like humans, can be tested for allergens. Discuss the testing with your veterinary dermatologist.

Long-coated dogs like the Beardie tend to be more susceptible to skin and coat problems. A grass allergy can be the cause of your Beardie's excessive scratching on his limbs or nose.

FOOD PROBLEMS

FOOD ALLERGIES

Dogs are allergic to many foods that are best-sellers and highly recommended by breeders and veterinary surgeons. Changing the brand of food that you buy may not eliminate the problem if the element to which the dog is allergic is contained in the new brand.

Recognising a food allergy is difficult. Humans vomit or have rashes when they eat a food to which they are allergic. Dogs neither vomit nor (usually) develop a rash. They react in the same manner as they do to an airborne or flea allergy: they itch, scratch and bite. Thus making the diagnosis extremely difficult. Whilst pollen allergies and parasite bites are usually seasonal, food allergies are year-round problems.

FOOD INTOLERANCE

Food intolerance is the inability of the dog to completely digest certain foods. Puppies that may have done very well on their mother's milk may not do well on cow's milk. The result of this food intolerance may be loose bowels, passing gas and stomach pains. These are the only obvious symptoms of food intolerance and that makes diagnosis difficult.

TREATING FOOD PROBLEMS

It is possible to handle food allergies and food intolerance yourself. Put your dog on a diet that it has never had. Obviously if it has never eaten this new food it can't have been allergic or intolerant of it. Start with a single ingredient that is not in the dog's diet at the present time. Ingredients like chopped beef or fish are common in dog's diets, so try something more exotic like rabbit, pheasant or even just vegetables. Keep the dog on this diet (with no additives) for a month. If the symptoms of food allergy or intolerance disappear, chances are your dog has a food allergy.

Don't think that the single ingredient cured the problem. You still must find a suitable diet and ascertain which ingredient in the old diet was objectionable. This is most easily done by adding ingredients to the new diet one at a time. Let the dog stay on the modified diet for a month before you add another ingredient. Eventually, you will determine the ingredient that caused the adverse reaction.

An alternative method is to carefully study the ingredients in the diet to which your dog is allergic or intolerant. Identify the main ingredient in this diet and eliminate the main ingredient by buying a different food that does not have that ingredient. Keep experimenting until the symptoms disappear after one month on the new diet.

A scanning electron micrograph (S. E. M.) of a dog flea, *Ctenocephalides canis.*

S. E. M. BY DR DENNIS KUNKEL, UNIVERSITY OF HAWAII

Opposite page: A scanning electron micrograph of a dog or cat flea, *Ctenocephalides,* magnified more than 100x. This has been colourised for effect.

EXTERNAL PARASITES

Of all the problems to which dogs are prone, none is more well known and frustrating than fleas. Flea infestation is relatively simple to cure but difficult to prevent. Parasites that are harboured

Magnified head of a dog flea, *Ctenocephalides canis.*

DID YOU KNOW?

Fleas have been around for millions of years and have adapted to changing host animals.

They are able to go through a complete life cycle in less than one month or they can extend their lives to almost two years by remaining as pupae or cocoons. They do not need blood or any other food for up to 20 months.

They have been measured as being able to jump 300,000 times and can jump 150 times their length in any direction including straight up. Those are just a few of the reasons they are so successful in infesting a dog!

inside the body are a bit more difficult to eradicate but they are easier to control.

FLEAS

To control a flea infestation you have to understand the flea's life cycle. Fleas are often thought of as a summertime problem but centrally heated homes have changed the patterns and fleas can be found at any time of the year. The most effective method of flea control is a two-stage approach: one stage to kill the adult fleas, and the other to control the development of pre-adult fleas. Unfortunately, no single active ingredient is effective against all stages of the life cycle.

LIFE CYCLE STAGES

During its life, a flea will pass through four life stages: egg, larva, pupa and adult. The adult stage is the most visible and irritating stage of the flea life

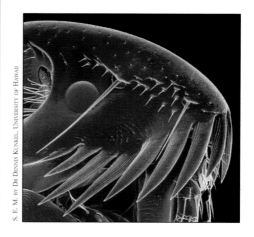

S. E. M. BY DR DENNIS KUNKEL, UNIVERSITY OF HAWAII

S. E. M. BY DR DENNIS KUNKEL, UNIVERSITY OF HAWAII

The Life Cycle of the Flea

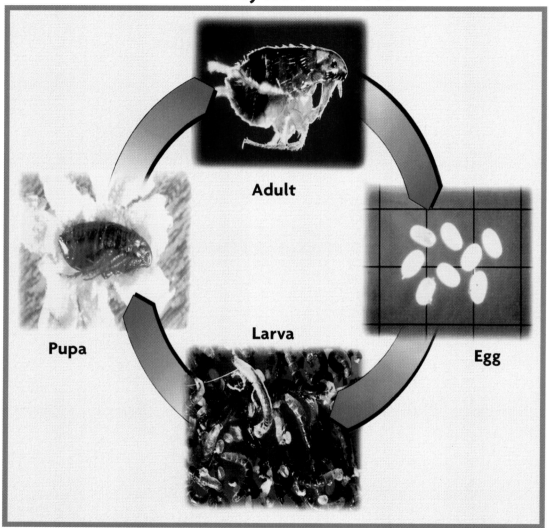

Adult

Pupa

Larva

Egg

The life cycle of the flea was posterised by Fleabusters®. Poster courtesy of Fleabusters®, R$_x$ for Fleas.

cycle and this is why the majority of flea-control products concentrate on this stage. The fact is that adult fleas account for only 1% of the total flea population, and the other 99% exist in pre-adult stages, i.e., eggs, larvae and pupae. The pre-adult stages are barely visible to the naked eye.

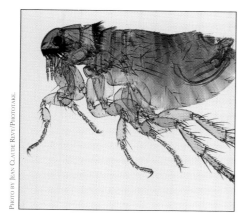

PHOTO BY JEAN CLAUDE REVY/PHOTOTAKE.

THE LIFE CYCLE OF THE FLEA

Eggs are laid on the dog, usually in quantities of about 20 or 30, several times a day. The female adult flea must have a blood meal before each egg-laying session. When first laid, the eggs will cling to the dog's fur, as the eggs are still moist. However, they will quickly dry out and fall from the dog, especially if the dog moves around or scratches. Many eggs will fall off in the dog's favourite area or an area in which

ON GUARD: CATCHING FLEAS OFF GUARD

Consider the following ways to arm yourself against fleas:

• Add a small amount of pennyroyal or eucalyptus oil to your dog's bath. These natural remedies repel fleas.

• Supplement your dog's food with fresh garlic (minced or grated) and a hearty amount of brewer's yeast, both of which ward off fleas.

• Use a flea comb on your dog daily. Submerge fleas in a cup of bleach to kill them quickly.

• Confine the dog to only a few rooms to limit the spread of fleas in the home.

• Vacuum daily...and get all of the crevices! Dispose of the bag every few days until the problem is under control.

• Wash your dog's bedding daily. Cover cushions where your dog sleeps with towels, and wash the towels often.

A male dog flea, *Ctenocephalides canis.*

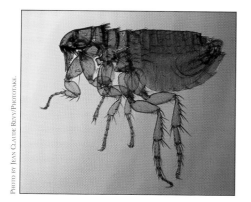

PHOTO BY JEAN CLAUDE REVY/PHOTOTAKE.

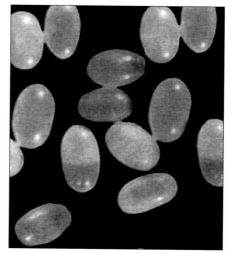

The eggs of the dog flea.

Male cat fleas, *Ctenocephalides felis,* **are very commonly found on dogs.**

125

he spends a lot of time, such as his bed.

Once the eggs fall from the dog onto the carpet or furniture, they will hatch into larvae. This takes from one to ten days. Larvae are not particularly mobile, and will usually travel only a few inches from where they hatch. However, they do have a tendency to move away from light and heavy traffic—under furniture and behind doors are common places to find high quantities of flea larvae.

The flea larvae feed on dead organic matter, including adult flea faeces, until they are ready to change into adult fleas. Fleas will usually remain as larvae for around seven days. After this period, the larvae will pupate into protective pupae. While inside the pupae, the larvae will undergo metamorphosis and change into

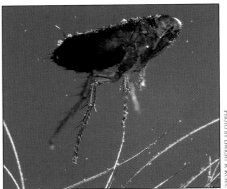

PHOTO BY DWIGHT R KUHN.

adult fleas. This can take as little time as a few days, but the adult fleas can remain inside the pupae waiting to hatch for up to two years. The pupae are signalled to hatch by certain stimuli, such as physical pressure—the pupae's being stepped on, heat from an animal lying on the pupae or increased carbon dioxide levels and vibrations—indicating that a suitable host is available.

Once hatched, the adult flea must feed within a few days. Once the adult flea finds a host, it will not leave voluntarily. It only becomes dislodged by grooming or the host animal's scratching. The adult flea will remain on the host for the duration of its life unless forcibly removed.

TREATING THE ENVIRONMENT AND THE DOG

Treating fleas should be a two-pronged attack. First, the environment needs to be treated; this includes carpets and furniture,

PHOTO BY DWIGHT R KUHN.

DID YOU KNOW?

Never mix flea control products without first consulting your veterinary surgeon. Some products can become toxic when combined with others and can cause serious or fatal consequences.

especially the dog's bedding and areas underneath furniture. The environment should be treated with a household spray containing an Insect Growth Regulator (IGR) and an insecticide to kill the adult fleas. Most IGRs are effective against eggs and larvae; they actually mimic the fleas' own hormones and stop the eggs and larvae from developing into adult fleas. There are currently no treatments available to attack the pupa stage of the life cycle, so the adult insecticide is used to kill the newly hatched adult fleas before they find a host. Most IGRs are active for many months, whilst adult insecticides are only active for a few days.

When treating with a household spray, it is a good idea to vacuum before applying the product. This stimulates as many pupae as possible to hatch into adult fleas. The vacuum cleaner should also be treated with a flea treatment to prevent the eggs and larvae that have been hoovered into the vacuum bag from hatching.

The second stage of treatment is to apply an adult insecticide to the dog. Traditionally, this would be in the form of a collar or a spray, but more recent innovations include digestible insecticides that poison the fleas when they ingest the dog's blood. Alternatively, there are drops that, when placed on the back of the animal's neck, spread throughout the fur and skin to kill adult fleas.

DID YOU KNOW?

Two types of products should be used when treating fleas—a product to treat the pet and a product to treat the home. Adult fleas represent less than 1% of the flea population. The pre-adult fleas (eggs, larvae and pupae) represent more than 99% of the flea population and are found in the environment; it is in the case of pre-adult fleas that products containing an Insect Growth Regulator (IGR) should be used in the home.

IGRs are a new class of compounds used to prevent the development of insects. They do not kill the insect outright, but instead use the insect's biology against it to stop it from completing its growth. Products that contain methoprene are the world's first and leading IGRs. Used to control fleas and other insects, this type of IGR will stop flea larvae from developing and protect the house for up to seven months.

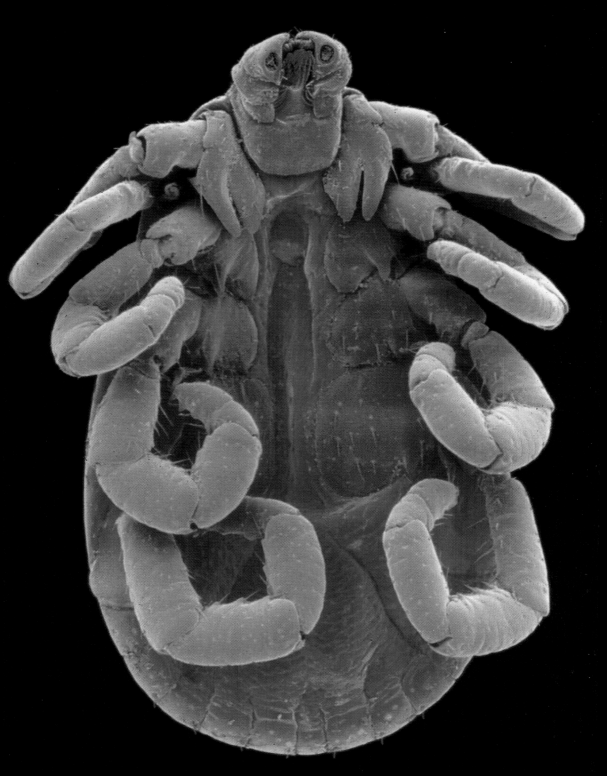

TICKS AND MITES

Though not as common as fleas, ticks and mites are found all over the tropical and temperate world. They don't bite, like fleas; they harpoon. They dig their sharp proboscis (nose) into the dog's skin and drink the blood. Their only food and drink is dog's blood. Dogs can get Lyme disease, Rocky Mountain spotted fever (normally found in the USA only), paralysis and many other diseases from ticks and mites. They may live where fleas are found and they like to hide in cracks or seams in walls wherever dogs live. They are controlled the same way fleas are controlled.

The dog tick, *Dermacentor variabilis*, may well be the most common dog tick in many geographical areas, especially those areas where the climate is hot and humid.

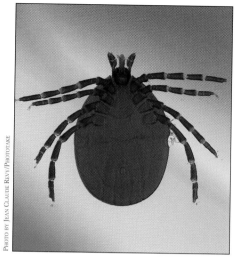

PHOTO BY JEAN CLAUDE REVY/PHOTOTAKE

Most dog ticks have life expectancies of a week to six months, depending upon climatic conditions. They can neither jump nor fly, but they can crawl slowly and can range up to 5 metres (16 feet) to reach a sleeping or unsuspecting dog.

MANGE

Mites cause a skin irritation called mange. Some are contagious, like *Cheyletiella*, ear mites, scabies and chiggers. The non-contagious mites are *Demodex*. Mites that cause ear-mite infestation are usually controlled with ivermectin, which is often toxic to Collies and probably should be avoided in all herding breeds.

It is essential that your dog be treated for mange as quickly as possible because some forms of mange are transmissible to people.

An uncommon dog tick of the genus *Ixode*. Magnified 10x.

Opposite page: The dog tick, *Dermacentor variabilis*, is probably the most common tick found on dogs. Look at the strength in its eight legs! No wonder it's hard to detach them.

A brown dog tick, *Rhipicephalus sanguineus*, is an uncommon but annoying tick found on dogs.

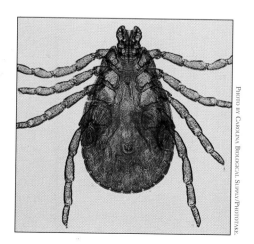

PHOTO BY CAROLINA BIOLOGICAL SUPPLY/PHOTOTAKE.

S E M BY DR DENNIS KUNKEL, UNIVERSITY OF HAWAII

129

Two views of the mange mite, *Psoroptes bovis.*

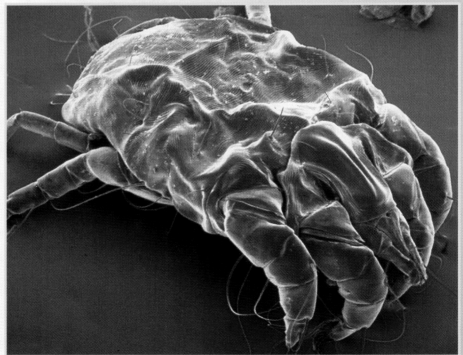

INTERNAL PARASITES

Most animals—fishes, birds and mammals, including dogs and humans—have worms and other parasites that live inside their bodies. According to Dr Herbert R Axelrod, the fish pathologist, there are two kinds of parasites: dumb and smart. The smart parasites live in peaceful coopera-tion with their hosts (symbiosis), while the dumb parasites kill their host. Most of the worm infections are relatively easy to control. If they are not controlled they eventually weaken the host dog to the point that other medical problems occur, but they are not dumb parasites.

ROUNDWORMS

The roundworms that infect dogs are scientifically known as *Toxocara canis*. They live in the dog's intestine. The worms shed eggs continually. It has been estimated that a dog produces about 150 grammes of faeces every day. Each gramme of faeces averages 10,000–12,000 eggs of roundworms. There are no known areas in which dogs roam that do not contain roundworm eggs. The greatest danger of roundworms is

> **DID YOU KNOW?**
>
> Ridding your puppy of worms is VERY IMPORTANT because certain worms that puppies carry, such as tapeworms and roundworms, can infect humans.
>
> Breeders initiate a deworming programme at or about four weeks of age. The routine is repeated every two or three weeks until the puppy is three months old. The breeder from whom you obtained your puppy should provide you with the complete details of the deworming programme.
>
> Your veterinary surgeon can prescribe and monitor the programme of deworming for you. The usual programme is treating the puppy every 15–20 days until the puppy is positively worm free.
>
> It is not advised that you treat your puppy with drugs that are not recommended professionally.

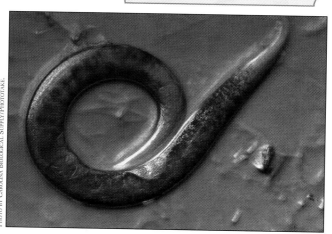

PHOTO BY CAROLINA BIOLOGICAL SUPPLY/PHOTOTAKE.

The roundworm, *Rhabditis*. The roundworm can infect both dogs and humans.

The roundworm *Rhabditis*.

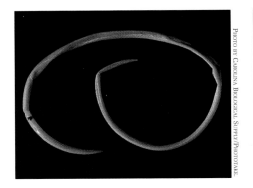

Photo by Carolina Biological Supply/Phototake.

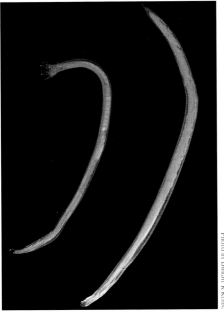

Photo by Dwight R Kuhn.

Male and female hookworms, *Ancylostoma caninum*, are uncommonly found in pet or show dogs in Britain. Hookworms may infect other dogs that have exposure to grasslands.

that they infect people too! It is wise to have your dog tested regularly for roundworms.

Pigs also have roundworm infections that can be passed to humans and dogs. The typical roundworm parasite is called *Ascaris lumbricoides*.

HOOKWORMS

The worm *Ancylostoma caninum* is commonly called the dog hookworm. It is dangerous to humans and cats. It also has teeth

by which it attaches itself to the intestines of the dog. It changes the site of its attachment about six times a day and the dog loses blood from each detachment, possibly causing iron-deficiency anaemia. Hookworms are easily purged from the dog with many medications. Milbemycin oxime, which also serves as a heartworm preventative in Collies, can be used for this purpose.

In Britain the 'temperate climate' hookworm (*Uncinaria stenocephala*) is rarely found in pet or show dogs, but can occur in hunting packs, racing Greyhounds and sheepdogs because the worms can be prevalent wherever dogs are exercised regularly on grassland.

DID YOU KNOW?

Caring for the puppy starts before the puppy is born by keeping the dam healthy and well-nourished. Most puppies have worms, even if they are not evident, so a worming programme is essential. The worms continually shed eggs except during their dormant stage, when they just rest in the tissues of the puppy. During this stage they are not evident during a routine examination.

DID YOU KNOW?

Average size dogs can pass 1,360,000 roundworm eggs every day.

For example, if there were only 1 million dogs in the world, the world would be saturated with 1,300 metric tonnes of dog faeces.

These faeces would contain 15,000,000,000 roundworm eggs.

7–31% of home gardens and children's play boxes in the U. S. contain roundworm eggs.

Flushing dog's faeces down the toilet is not a safe practice because the usual sewage treatments do not destroy roundworm eggs.

Infected puppies start shedding roundworm eggs at 3 weeks of age. They can be infected by their mother's milk.

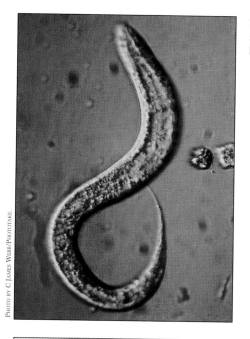

PHOTO BY C JAMES WEBB/PHOTOTAKE.

The infective stage of the hookworm larva.

TAPEWORMS

There are many species of tapeworms. They are carried by fleas! The dog eats the flea and starts the tapeworm cycle. Humans can also be infected with tapeworms, so don't eat fleas! Fleas are so small that your dog could pass them onto your hands, your plate or your food and thus make it possible for you to ingest a flea which is carrying tapeworm eggs.

While tapeworm infection is not life threatening in dogs (smart parasite!), it can be the cause of a very serious liver disease for humans. About 50 percent of the humans infected with

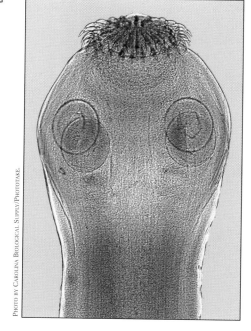

PHOTO BY CAROLINA BIOLOGICAL SUPPLY/PHOTOTAKE.

The head and rostellum (the round prominence on the scolex) of a tapeworm, which infects dogs and humans.

Echinococcus multilocularis, a type of tapeworm that causes alveolar hydatis, perish.

HEARTWORMS

Heartworms are thin, extended worms up to 30 cms (12 ins) long which live in a dog's heart and the major blood vessels surrounding it. Dogs may have up to 200 of these worms. The symptoms may be loss of energy, loss of appetite, coughing, the development of a pot belly and anaemia.

Heartworms are transmitted by mosquitoes. The mosquito drinks the blood of an infected dog and takes in larvae with the blood. The larvae, called microfilaria, develop within the body of the mosquito and are passed on to the next dog bitten after the larvae mature. It takes two to three weeks for the larvae to develop to the infective stage within the body of the mosquito. Dogs should be treated at about six weeks of age, then every six months.

> **DID YOU KNOW?**
>
> Humans, rats, squirrels, foxes, coyotes, wolves, mixed breeds of dogs and purebred dogs are all susceptible to tapeworm infection. Except in humans, tapeworms are usually not a fatal infection.
>
> Infected individuals can harbour a thousand parasitic worms.
>
> Tapeworms have two sexes—male and female (many other worms have only one sex—male and female in the same worm).
>
> If dogs eat infected rats or mice, they get the tapeworm disease.
>
> One month after attaching to a dog's intestine, the worm starts shedding eggs. These eggs are infective immediately.
>
> Infective eggs can live for a few months without a host animal.
>
> Roundworms, whipworms and tapeworms are just a few of the other commonly known worms that infect dogs.

Blood testing for heartworms is not necessarily indicative of how seriously your dog is infected. This is a dangerous disease. Although heartworm is a problem for dogs in America, Australia, Asia and Central Europe, dogs in the United Kingdom are not affected by heartworm.

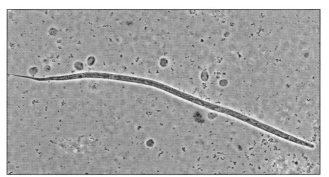

The heartworm, *Dirofilaria immitis*.

PHOTO BY JAMES E HAYDEN, RPB/PHOTOTAKE .

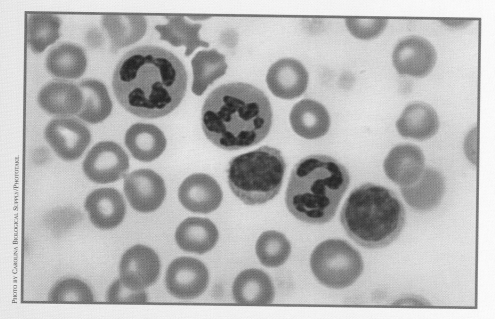

Magnified heartworm larvae, *Dirofilaria immitis.*

The heart of a dog infected with canine heartworm, *Dirofilaria immitis.*

When you purchased your Bearded Collie you will have made it clear to the breeder whether you wanted one just as a loveable companion and pet, or if you hoped to be buying a Bearded Collie with show prospects. No reputable breeder will have sold you a young puppy saying that it was definitely of show quality for so much can go wrong during the early months of a puppy's development. If you plan to show what you will hopefully have acquired is a puppy with 'show potential.'

To the novice, exhibiting a Bearded Collie in the show ring may look easy but it usually takes a lot of hard work and devotion to do top winning at a show such as the prestigious Crufts, not to mention a little luck too!

The first concept that the

canine novice learns when watching a dog show is that each breed first competes against members of its own breed. Once the judge has selected the best member of each breed, provided that the show is judged on a Group system, that chosen dog will compete with other dogs in its group. Finally the best of each group will compete for Best in Show and Reserve Best in Show.

The second concept that you must understand is that the dogs are not actually competing against one another. The judge compares each dog against the breed standard, which is a written description of the ideal specimen of the breed. Whilst some early breed standards were indeed based on specific dogs that were famous or popular, many dedicated enthusiasts say that a perfect specimen, described in the standard, has never walked into a show ring, has never been bred and, to the woe of dog breeders around the globe, does not exist. Breeders attempt to get as close to this ideal as possible, with every litter, but theoretically the 'perfect' dog is so elusive that it is impossible. (And if the 'perfect'

DID YOU KNOW?
The Kennel Club divides its dogs into seven Groups: Gundogs, Utility, Working, Toy, Terrier, Hounds and Pastoral.*

*The Pastoral Group, established in 1999, includes those sheepdog breeds previously categorised in the Working Group.

dog were born, breeders and judges would never agree that it was indeed 'perfect.')

If you are interested in exploring dog shows, your best bet is to join your local breed club. These clubs often host both Championship and Open Shows, and sometimes Match meetings and special events, all of which could be of interest, even if you are only an onlooker. Clubs also send out newsletters and some organise training days and seminars in order that people may learn more about their chosen breed. To locate the nearest breed club for you, contact The Kennel Club, the ruling body for the British dog world. The Kennel Club governs not only conformation shows but also working trials, obedience trials, agility trials and field trials. The Kennel Club furnishes the rules and regulations for all these events plus general dog registration and other basic requirements of dog ownership. Its annual show called the Crufts Dogs Show, held in Birmingham, is the largest benched show in England. Every year over 20,000 of the UK's best dogs qualify to participate in this marvellous show which lasts four days.

The Kennel Club governs many different kinds of shows in Great Britain, Australia, South Africa and beyond. At the most competitive and prestigious of these shows, the Championship Shows, a dog can

If you are interested in showing your Bearded Collie, it would be a good idea to go to one or two shows in order to get a feel for what goes on and how show dogs look and act.

earn Challenge Certificates, and thereby become a Show Champion or a Champion. A dog must earn three Challenge Certificates under three different judges to earn the prefix of 'Sh Ch' or 'Ch.' Note that some breeds must also qualify in a

WINNING THE TICKET
Earning a championship at Kennel Club shows is the most difficult in the world. Compared to the United States and Canada where it is relatively not 'challenging,' collecting three green tickets not only requires much time and effort, it can be very expensive! Challenge Certificates, as the tickets are properly known, are the building blocks of champions—good breeding, good handling, good training and good luck!

field trial in order to gain the title of full champion. Challenge Certificates are awarded to a very small percentage of the dogs competing, especially as dogs that are already Champions compete with others for these coveted CCs. The number of Challenge Certificates awarded in any one year is based upon the total number of dogs in each breed entered for competition.

There are three types of Championship Shows: an all-breed General Championship Show for all Kennel-Club-recognised breeds; a Group Championship Show, limited to breeds within one of the Groups; and a Breed Show, usually confined to a single breed. The Kennel Club determines which breeds at which Championship Shows will have the opportunity to earn Challenge Certificates (or tickets). Serious exhibitors often will opt not to participate if the tickets are withheld at a particular show. This policy makes earning championships ever more difficult to accomplish.

Open Shows are generally less competitive and are frequently used as 'practice shows' for young dogs. There are hundreds of Open Shows each year that can be invitingly social events and are great first show experiences for the novice. Even if you're considering just watching a show to wet your paws, an Open Show is a great choice.

Whilst Championship and Open Shows are most important for the beginner to understand, there are other types of shows in which the interested dog owner can participate. Training clubs sponsor Matches that can be entered on the day of the show for a nominal fee. In these introductory-level exhibitions, two dogs are pulled out of a hat and 'matched,' the winner of that match goes on to the next round, and eventually only one dog is left undefeated.

SHOW RING ETIQUETTE

Just as with anything else, there is a certain etiquette to the show ring that can only be learned through experience. Showing your dog can be quite intimidating to you as a novice when it seems as if everyone else knows what they are doing. You can familiarise yourself with ring procedure beforehand by taking a class to prepare you and your dog for conformation showing or by talking with an experienced handler. When you are in the ring, listen and pay attention to the judge and follow his/her directions. Remember, even the most skilled handlers had to start somewhere. Keep it up and you too will become a proficient handler before too long!

Exemption Shows are much more light-hearted affairs with usually only four pedigree classes and several 'fun' classes, all of which can be entered on the day. The proceeds of an Exemption Show must be given to a charity and are sometimes held in conjunction with small agricultural shows. Limited Shows are also available in small number, but entry is restricted to members of the club which hosts the show, although one can usually join the club when making an entry.

Before you actually step into the ring, you would be well advised to sit back and observe the judge's ring procedure. If it is your first time in the ring, do not be over-anxious and run to the front of the line. It is much better to stand back and study how the exhibitor in front of you is performing. The judge asks each handler to 'stand' the dog, hopefully showing the dog off to his best advantage. The judge will observe the dog from a distance and from different angles, approach the dog, check his teeth, overall structure, alertness and muscle tone, as well as consider how well the dog 'conforms' to the standard. Most importantly, the judge will have the exhibitor move the dog around the ring in some pattern that he or she should specify (another advantage to not going first, but always listen since some judges change their

An historical win for a Bearded Collie at the Crufts Dog Show. This Bearded Collie won Best of Breed and was the first dog ever to win the newly designated Pastoral Group in 1999.

directions, and the judge is always right!) Finally the judge will give the dog one last look before moving on to the next exhibitor.

If you are not in the top three at your first show, do not be discouraged. Be patient and consistent and you may eventually find yourself in the winning line-up. Remember that the winners were once in your shoes and have devoted many hours and much money to earn the placement. If you find that your dog is losing every time and never getting a nod, it may be time to consider a different dog sport or just enjoy your Bearded Collie as a pet.

As a Bearded Collie owner, you have selected your dog so that you and your loved ones can have a companion, a protector, a friend and a four-legged family member. You invest time, money and effort to care for and train the family's new charge. Of course, this chosen canine behaves perfectly! Well, perfectly like a dog.

THINK LIKE A DOG

Dogs do not think like humans, nor do humans think like dogs, though we try. Unfortunately, a dog is incapable of compre-hending how humans think, so the responsibility falls on the owner to adopt a proper canine mindset. Dogs cannot rationalise, and dogs exist in the present moment. Many dog owners make the mistake in training of thinking that they can reprimand their dog for something he did a while ago. Basically, you cannot even reprimand a dog for something he did 20 seconds ago! Either catch him in the act or forget it! It is a waste of your and your dog's time—in his mind, you are reprimanding him for whatever he is doing at that moment.

The following behavioural problems represent some which owners most commonly encounter. Every dog is unique and every situation is unique. No author could purport to solve your Bearded Collie's problems simply by reading a script. Here we outline some basic 'dogspeak' so that owners' chances of solving behavioural problems are increased. Discuss bad habits with your veterinary surgeon and he/she can recommend a behavioural specialist to consult in appropriate cases. Since behavioural abnormalities are the leading reason owners abandon their pets, we hope that you will make a valiant effort to solve your Bearded Collie's problems. Patience and understanding are virtues that dwell in every pet-loving household.

DID YOU KNOW?

Your dog inherited the pack-leader mentality. He only knows about pecking order. He instinctively wants to be top dog but you have to convince him that you are boss. There is no such thing as living in a democracy with your dog. You are the dictator, the absolute monarch.

JUMPING UP

For the Beardie, jumping up is more than friendly way of saying hello—it is an essential way of life! Some dog owners do not mind when their Beardies jump up, loving every furry kilogram! Nonetheless, a problem arises when guests come to the house and the dog greets them in the same manner—whether they like it or not. However friendly the greeting may be, the chances are that your visitors will not appreciate your dog's bouncing, boundless enthusiasm. The dog will not be able to distinguish upon whom he can jump and whom he cannot. Therefore, it is probably best to discourage this behaviour entirely.

Pick a command such as 'Off.' (avoid using 'Down' since you will use that for the dog to lie down) and tell him 'Off' when he jumps up. Place him on the ground on all fours and have him sit, praising him the whole time. Always lavish him with praise and petting when he is in the sit position. That way you are still giving him a warm affectionate greeting, because you are as excited to see him as he is to see you!

BARKING

Giving voice, aka barking, is a bred-for characteristic of the working Bearded Collie. As the Beardie herds his fleecy charges,

Beardies can be the most exuberant greeters in the dog world, hence owners frequently have problems with their full-grown Beardies jumping up on children and strangers. This behaviour must be curtailed from puppyhood.

141

he instinctively gives voice, communicating with both the sheep and his master (the shepherd). There is no doubt that every Beardie has a lot to say—regardless of whether he's been asked. Whatever it is that the dog is trying to say, he should not be punished for barking.

In our modern societies, where Beardies rarely herd anything more impressive or useful than children and bedroom slippers, a barky Beardie is not desirable. It will be necessary to redirect the Beardie pup's barking from the very beginning, or else your Beardie might be hosting his own talkshow in no time at all...and your neighbours will not tune in with much amusement.

Fortunately, Beardies tend to use their barks more purposefully

DID YOU KNOW?
Dogs get to know each other by sniffing each other's backsides. It seems that each dog has a telltale odour probably created by the anal glands. It also distinguishes sex and signals when a female will be receptive to a male's attention. Some dog's snap at the other dog's intrusion of their private parts.

than most dogs, and thereby can be taught when to bark and when not to bark. If an intruder came into your home in the middle of the night and your Bearded Collie barked a warning, wouldn't you be pleased? You would probably deem your dog a hero, a wonderful guardian and protector of the home. Most dogs are not as discriminate as the Bearded Collie. For instance, if a friend drops by unexpectedly and rings the doorbell and is greeted with a sudden sharp bark, you would probably be annoyed at the dog. But in reality, isn't this just the same behaviour? The dog does not know any better...unless he sees who is at the door and it is someone he knows, he will bark as a means of vocalising that his (and your) territory is being threatened. Whilst your friend is not posing a threat, it is all the same to the dog. Barking is his means of letting you know that there is an intrusion, whether

DID YOU KNOW?
To encourage proper barking, you can teach your dog the command 'quiet.' When someone comes to the door and the dog barks a few times, praise him. Talk to him soothingly and when he stops barking, tell him 'quiet' and continue to praise him. In this sense you are letting him bark his warning, which is an instinctive behaviour, and then rewarding him for being quiet after a few barks. You may initially reward him with a treat after he has been quiet for a few minutes.

friend or foe, on your property. This type of barking is instinctive and should not be discouraged. Let your Beardie know when his bark is appropriate and when it is not.

Excessive habitual barking, however, is a problem that should be corrected early on. As your Bearded Collie grows up, you will be able to tell when his barking is purposeful and when it is for no reason. You will become able to distinguish your dog's different barks and their meanings. For example, the bark when someone comes to the door will be different from the bark when he is excited to see you. It is similar to a person's tone of voice, except that the dog has to rely totally on tone of voice because he does not have the benefit of using words. An incessant barker will be evident at an early age.

There are some things that encourage a dog to bark. For example, if your dog barks non-

stop for a few minutes and you give him a treat to quieten him, he believes that you are rewarding him for barking. He will associate barking with getting a treat, and will keep doing it until he is rewarded.

AGGRESSION

Aggression can be a very big problem in dogs, but more so in breeds with a fighting background, which is not a factor with the Beardie. Aggression, when not controlled, always becomes dangerous. An aggressive dog, no matter the size, may lunge at, bite or even attack a person or another dog. Aggressive behaviour is not to be tolerated.

DID YOU KNOW?

We all love our dogs and our dogs love us. They show their love and affection by licking us. This is not a

very sanitary practice as dogs lick and sniff in some unsavory places. Kissing your dog on the mouth is strictly forbidden, as parasites can be transmitted in this manner.

Whilst not all aggressive behaviour is dangerous, growling, baring teeth, etc., can be frightening. It is important to ascertain why the dog is acting in this manner. Aggression is a display of dominance, and the dog should not have the dominant role in its pack, which is, in this case, your family.

It is important not to challenge an aggressive dog as this could provoke an attack. Observe your Bearded Collie's body language. Does he make direct eye contact and stare? Does he try to make himself as large as possible: ears alert, chest out, tail erect? Height and size signify authority in a dog pack—being taller or 'above' another dog

literally means that he is 'above' in the social status. These body signals tell you that your Bearded Collie thinks he is in charge, a problem that needs to be addressed. An aggressive dog is unpredictable: you never know when he is going to strike and what he is going to do. You cannot understand why a dog that is playful one minute is growling the next.

The best solution is to consult a behavioural specialist, one who has experience with the Bearded Collie if possible. Together, perhaps you can pinpoint the cause of your dog's aggression and do something about it. An aggressive dog cannot be trusted, and a dog that cannot be trusted is not safe to have as a family pet. If, very unusually, you find that your pet has become untrustworthy and you feel it necessary to seek a new home with a more suitable family and environment, explain fully to the new owners all your reasons for re-homing the dog to

DID YOU KNOW?

Dog aggression is a serious problem. NEVER give an aggressive dog to someone else. The dog will usually be more aggressive in a new situation where his leadership is unchallenged and unquestioned (in his mind).

be fair to all concerned. In the very worst case, you will have to consider euthanasia.

DOMINANT AGGRESSION

A social hierarchy is firmly established in a wild dog pack. The dog wants to dominate those under him and please those above him. Dogs know that there must be a leader. If you are not the obvious choice for emperor, the dog will assume the throne! These conflicting innate desires are what a dog owner is up against when he sets about training a dog. In training a dog to obey commands, the owner is reinforcing that he is the top dog in the 'pack' and that the dog should, and should want to, serve his superior. Thus, the owner is suppressing the dog's urge to dominate by modifying his behaviour and making him obedient.

An important part of training is taking every opportunity to reinforce that you are the leader.

By making your Beardie wait for his food in his crate, you are reinforcing your dominance and top-dog status. This device proves most helpful with dogs with dominant or aggressive tendencies.

The simple action of making your Bearded Collie sit to wait for his food says that you control when he eats and that he is dependent on you for food. Although it may be difficult, do not give in to your dog's wishes every time he whines at you or looks at you with his pleading eyes. It is a constant effort to show the dog that his place in the pack is at the bottom. This is not meant to sound cruel or inhumane. You love your Bearded Collie and you should treat him with care and affection. You (hopefully) did not get a dog just so you could boss about another creature. Dog training is not about being cruel

DID YOU KNOW?

If you are approached by an aggressive, growling dog, do not run away. Simply stand still and avoid eye contact. If you have something in your hand (like a handbag), throw it sideways away from your body to distract the dog from making a frontal attack.

145

Beardies generally enjoy the company of cats, especially if socialised with them from puppyhood. More often, the cat doesn't trust the Beardie because of its boisterous, unruly nature.

reward him for it. Add a dog into the equation and it becomes a bit more trying, but as a rule of thumb, positive reinforcement is what works best.

With a dominant dog, punishment and negative reinforcement can have the opposite effect from what you desire. It can make a dog fearful and/or act out aggressively if he feels he is being challenged. Remember, a

Keep your Bearded Collie on a leash so that you are able to control him if you encounter another dog. If puppies are properly socialised with other dogs, there shouldn't be a problem...but you never know about someone else's dog.

or feeling important, it is about moulding the dog's behaviour into what is acceptable and teaching him to live by your rules. In theory, it is quite simple: catch him in appropriate behaviour and

dominant dog perceives himself at the top of the social heap and will fight to defend his perceived status. The best way to prevent that is never to give him reason to think that he is in control in the first place. If you are having trouble training your Bearded Collie and it seems as if he is constantly challenging your authority, seek the help of an obedience trainer or behavioural specialist. A professional will work with both you and your dog to teach you effective techniques to use at home. Beware of trainers who rely on excessively harsh methods; scolding is necessary now and then, but the focus in your training should always be on positive reinforcement.

DID YOU KNOW?
Fear in a grown dog is often the result of improper or incomplete socialisation as a pup, or it can be the result of a traumatic experience he suffered when young. Keep in mind that the term 'traumatic' is relative—something that you would not think twice about can leave a lasting negative impression on a puppy. If the dog experiences a similar experience later in life, he may try to fight back to protect himself. Again, this behaviour is very unpredictable, especially if you do not know what is triggering his fear.

DID YOU KNOW?
When a dog bites there is always a good reason for it doing so. Many dogs are trained to protect a person, an area or an object. When that person, area or object is violated, the dog will attack. A dog attacks with its mouth. It has no other means of attack. It never uses teeth for defense. It merely runs away or lies down on the ground when it is in an indefensible situation. Fighting dogs (and there are many breeds which fight) are taught to fight, but they also have a natural instinct to fight. This instinct is normally reserved for other dogs, though unfortunate accidents occur when babies crawl towards a fighting dog and the dog mistakes the crawling child as a potential attacker.

If a dog is a biter for no reason, if it bites the hand that feeds it or if it snaps at members of your family, see your veterinary surgeon or behaviourist immediately to learn how to modify the dog's behaviour.

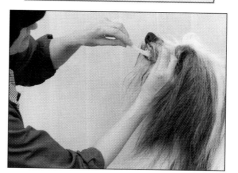

It is important that your Bearded Collie feels comfortable in all situations, grooming included, to avoid fear biting.

147

If you can isolate what brings out the fear reaction, you can help the dog overcome it. Supervise your Bearded Collie's interactions with people and other dogs, and praise the dog when it goes well. If he starts to act aggressively in a situation, correct him and remove him from the situation. Do not let people approach the dog and start petting him without your express permission. That way, you can have the dog sit to accept petting, and praise him when he behaves properly. You are focusing on praise and on modifying his behaviour by rewarding him when he acts appropriately. By being gentle and by supervising his interactions, you are showing him that there is no need to be afraid or defensive.

SEXUAL BEHAVIOUR

Dogs exhibit certain sexual behaviours that may have influenced your choice of male or female when you first purchased your Bearded Collie. To a certain extent, spaying/neutering will eliminate these behaviours, but if you are purchasing a dog that you wish to breed from, you should be aware of what you will have to deal with throughout the dog's life.

Female dogs usually have two oestruses per year with each season lasting about three weeks. These are the only times in which a female dog will mate, and she

Chewing can be a problem, especially if your dog starts to ruin your belongings. Provide proper chew toys for your Bearded Collie to encourage constructive chewing habits.

usually will not allow this until the second week of the cycle, but this does vary from bitch to bitch. If not bred during the heat cycle, it is not uncommon for a bitch to experience a false pregnancy, in which her mammary glands swell and she exhibits maternal tendencies toward toys or other objects.

Owners must further recognise that mounting is not merely a sexual expression but also one of dominance. Be consistent and persistent and you will find that you can 'move mounters.'

CHEWING

The national canine pastime is chewing! Every dog loves to sink his 'canines' into a tasty bone, but sometimes that bone is attached to his owner's hand! Dogs need to chew, to massage their gums, to make their new teeth feel better and to exercise their jaws. This is a natural behaviour deeply imbedded in all things canine. Our role as owners is not to stop the dog's chewing, but to redirect it to positive, chew-worthy objects. Be an informed owner and purchase proper chew toys like strong nylon bones that will not splinter. Be sure that the devices are safe and durable, since your dog's safety is at risk.

Again, the owner is responsible for ensuring a dog-proof environment. The best answer is prevention; that is, put your shoes, handbags and other tasty objects in their proper places (out of the reach of the growing canine mouth). Direct puppies to their toys whenever you see them tasting the furniture legs or the leg of your trousers. Make a loud noise to attract the pup's attention and immediately escort him to his chew toy and engage him with the toy for at least four minutes, praising and encouraging him all the while.

Some trainers recommend deterrents, such as hot pepper or another bitter spice or a product designed for this purpose, to discourage the dog from chewing unwanted objects. Test out these

DID YOU KNOW?

Punishment is rarely necessary for a misbehaving dog. Dogs that are habitually bad probably had a poor education and they do not know what is expected of them. They need training. Disciplinary behaviour on your part usually does more harm than good.

DID YOU KNOW?

Physical games like pulling contests, wrestling, jumping and teasing should not be encouraged. Inciting the dog's crazy behaviour tends to confuse a dog. The owner has to be able to control his dog at all times; even in play, your dog has to know you're the leader and you decide when to play and when to behave mannerly.

products yourself before investing in a large quantities.

DIGGING

Digging, which is seen as a destructive behaviour to humans, is actually quite a natural behaviour in dogs. Although your dog is not one of the 'earth dogs' (also known as terriers), his desire to dig can be irrepressible and most frustrating to his owners. When digging occurs in your garden, it is actually a normal behaviour redirected into something the dog can do in his everyday life. In the wild, a dog would be actively seeking food, making his own shelter, etc. He would be using his paws in a purposeful manner for his survival. Since you provide him with food and shelter, he has no need to use his paws for these purposes, and so the energy that he would be using may manifest itself in the form of little holes all

Food stealing can be a problem for Beardies that are underfed or are used to eating human food. This problem manifests itself not only at the dinner table, as begging, but in the dustbins as well.

over your garden and flower beds.

Perhaps your dog is digging as a reaction to boredom—it is somewhat similar to someone eating a whole bag of crisps in front of the TV—because they are there and there is not anything better to do! Basically, the answer is to provide the dog with adequate play and exercise so that his mind and paws are occupied, and so that he feels as if he is doing something useful.

Of course, digging is easiest to control if it is stopped as soon as possible, but it is often hard to catch a dog in the act. If your dog is a compulsive digger and is not easily distracted by other activi-

ties, you can designate an area on your property where it is okay for him to dig. If you catch him digging in an off-limits area of the garden, immediately bring him to the approved area and praise him for digging there. Keep a close eye on him so that you can catch him in the act— that is the only way to make him understand what is permitted and what is not. If you take him to a hole he dug an hour ago and tell him 'No,' he will understand that you are not fond of holes, or dirt, or flowers. If you catch him whilst he is stifle-deep in your tulips, that is when he will get your message.

151

FOOD STEALING

Is your dog devising ways of stealing food from your coffee table? If so, you must answer the following questions: Is your Bearded Collie hungry, or is he 'constantly famished' like many dogs seem to be? Face it, some dogs are more food-motivated than others. Some dogs are totally obsessed by the smell of food and can only think of their next meal. Food stealing is terrific fun and always yields a great reward—FOOD, glorious food.

The owner's goal, therefore, is to be sensible about where food is placed in the home, and to reprimand your dog whenever caught in the act of stealing. But remember, only reprimand the dog if you actually see him stealing, not later when the

> **DID YOU KNOW?**
> You should never play tug-of-war games with your puppy. Such games create a struggle for 'top dog' position and teach the puppy that it is okay to challenge you. It will also encourage your puppy's natural tendency to bite down hard and *win*.

> **DID YOU KNOW?**
> Never scream, shout, jump or run about if you want your dog to stay calm. You set the example for your dog's behaviour in most circumstances. Learn from your dog's reaction to your behaviour and act accordingly.

crime is discovered for that will be of no use at all and will only serve to confuse.

BEGGING

Just like food stealing, begging is a favourite pastime of hungry puppies! It yields that same lovely reward—FOOD! Dogs quickly learn that their owners keep the 'good food' for themselves, and that we humans do not dine on dried food alone. Begging is a conditioned response related to a specific stimulus, time and place. The sounds of the kitchen, cans and bottles opening, crinkling bags, the smell of food in preparation, etc., will excite the dog and soon the paws are in the air!

Here is the solution to stopping this behaviour: Never give in to a beggar! You are rewarding the dog for sitting pretty, jumping up, whining and rubbing his nose into you by giving him that glorious reward—food. By ignoring the dog, you will (eventually) force the behaviour into extinction. Note that the behaviour is likely to get worse before it disappears, so be sure there are not any 'softies' in the family who will give in to little 'Oliver' every time he whimpers, 'More, please.'

SEPARATION ANXIETY

Your Bearded Collie may howl, whine or otherwise vocalise his displeasure at your leaving the house and his being left alone. This is a normal reaction, no different from the child who cries as his mother leaves him on the first day at school. In fact, constant attention can lead to separation anxiety in the first place. If you are constantly making a fuss of your dog, he will come to expect this from you all of the time and it will be more traumatic for him when you are not there. Obviously, you enjoy spending time with

Your Bearded Collie loves your company. If dogs are left alone too much, they can suffer from separation anxiety.

your dog, and he thrives on your love and attention. However, it should not become a dependent relationship where he is heartbroken without you.

One thing you can do to minimise separation anxiety is to make your entrances and exits as low-key as possible. Do not give your dog a long drawn-out goodbye, and do not overly lavish him with hugs and kisses when you return. This is giving in to the attention that he craves, and it will only make him miss it more when you are away. Another thing you can try is to give your dog a treat when you leave; this will not only keep him occupied and keep his mind off the fact that you have just left, but it will also help him associate your leaving with a pleasant experience.

DID YOU KNOW?

Dogs left alone for varying lengths of time may often react wildly when you return. Sometimes they run, jump, bite, chew, tear things apart, wet themselves, gobble their food or behave in a very undisciplined manner. Allow them to calm down before greeting them or they will consider your attention as a reward for their antics.

Bearded Collies depend on the love and affection they receive from their human families.

Bearded Collies depend on the love and affection they receive from their human families.

You may have to accustom your dog to being left alone in intervals. Of course, when your dog starts whimpering as you approach the door, your first instinct will be to run to him and comfort him, but do not do it! Really—eventually he will adjust and be just fine if you take it in small steps. His anxiety stems from being placed in an unfamiliar situation; by familiarising him with being alone he will learn that he is okay. That is not to say you should purposely leave your dog home alone, but the dog needs to know that whilst he can depend on you for his care, you do not have to be by his side 24 hours a day.

When the dog is alone in the house, he should be confined to his designated dog-proof area of the house. This should be the area

DID YOU KNOW?

The number of dogs who suffer from separation anxiety is on the rise as more and more pet owners find themselves at work all day. New attention is being paid to this problem, which is especially hard to diagnose since it is only evident when the dog is alone. Research is currently being done to help educate dog owners about separation anxiety and how they can help minimise this problem in their dogs.

in which he sleeps and already feels comfortable so he will feel more at ease when he is alone.

COPROPHAGIA

Faeces eating is, to humans, one of the most disgusting behaviours that their dog could engage in, yet to the dog it is perfectly normal. It is hard for us to understand why a dog would want to eat its own faeces. He could be seeking certain nutrients that are missing from his diet; he could be just plain hungry; or he could be attracted by the pleasing (to a dog) scent. Whilst coprophagia most often refers to the dog eating his own faeces, a dog may just as likely eat that of another animal as well if he comes across it. Vets have found that diets with a low digestibility, containing relatively low levels of fibre and high levels of starch, increase coprophagia. Therefore, high-fibre diets may decrease the likelihood of dogs' eating faeces. Both the consistency of the stool (how firm it feels in the dog's mouth) and the presence of undigested nutrients increase the likelihood. Dogs often find the stool of cats and horses more palatable than that of other dogs. Once the dog develops diarrhoea from faeces eating, it will likely quit this distasteful habit.

To discourage this behaviour, first make sure that the food you are feeding your dog is nutrition-

Prevent coprophagia (stool eating) by making sure that you clean up after your dog every time he eliminates.

ally complete and that he is getting enough food. If changes in his diet do not seem to work, and no medical cause can be found, you will have to modify the behaviour before it becomes a habit through environmental control. The best way to prevent your dog from eating his stool is to make it unavailable—clean up after he eliminates and remove any stool from the garden. If it is not there, he cannot eat it.

Reprimanding for stool eating rarely impresses the dog. Vets recommend distracting the dog whilst he is in the act of stool eating. Coprophagia is seen most frequently in pups 6 to 12 months of age, and usually disappears around the dog's first birthday.

INDEX

*Page numbers in **boldface** indicate illustrations.*

My Bearded Collie

PUT YOUR PUPPY'S FIRST PICTURE HERE

Dog's Name _____

Date _____ Photographer _____